Praise for *The Recovering Body*

Jennifer Matesa's *The Recovering Body* is an engaging commentary on the importance of exercise and meditation for people in recovery—but it is so much more than simply a self-help book. Personal, luminous in its depth of understanding of the human condition, this is a book that would benefit anyone who struggles with self-image.

—Kaylie Jones, publisher of Kaylie Jones Books
and author of *Lies My Mother Never Told Me*

The Recovering Body is an essential read for anyone struggling with addiction and compulsion. Matesa has integrated science and stories that provide critical insight and guidance from every perspective. This book is *the* road map toward fulfillment and happiness.

—Shane Niemeyer, triathlete and author of
The Hurt Artist: My Journey from Suicidal Junkie to Ironman

With warmth and intelligence, Matesa suggests that healing the body from physical addiction is not separate from spiritual healing. Through fascinating stories from the field and using her experience as an educator and journalist who overcame her own addiction, she explains how movement, nourishment, sleep, pleasure, and mindfulness pave the road home to yourself. A blueprint for healing, body and soul.

—Susan Piver, author of *The Wisdom of a Broken Heart*

The
RECOVERING
BODY

The
RECOVERING
BODY

Physical and Spiritual Fitness for Living Clean and Sober

Jennifer Matesa

HAZELDEN®

Hazelden
Center City, Minnesota 55012
hazelden.org

ISBN: 978-1-61649-537-4

Library of Congress Cataloging-in-Publication Data is on file at the Library of Congress.

Editor's note
The names, details, and circumstances may have been changed to protect the privacy of those mentioned in this publication.

This publication is not intended as a substitute for the advice of health care professionals.

Alcoholics Anonymous, AA, and the Big Book are registered trademarks of Alcoholics Anonymous World Services, Inc.

18 17 16 15 14   1 2 3 4 5 6

Cover design: Theresa Jaeger Gedig
Developmental editor: Sid Farrar
Production editor: Jean Cook, ImageSmythe
Typesetting: Bookmobile Design & Digital Publisher Services

For Jonathan
for his honesty, guts, and wild sense of humor.
Live well, *hijito*.

Contents

Acknowledgments

My editor, Sid Farrar, and the team at Hazelden,
for requesting and believing in this work

My agent, Stephany Evans at Fine Print Literary,
for her excellent representation

All my sources quoted herein—my deepest gratitude for your time,
expertise, and stories, which are priceless

Von Keairns, Virginia Mayo and Elise Yoder, Kathy F. and Anita,
Chimene, Debbe, Jess, Kathie, Lori, Mary Jo, and Nancy,
Moira, Laurel, Jim Z., and my sister Judy, for unfailing love

Carole C. for the central metaphor of this book

Susan Atkinson and John Beiter, for listening and healing

Kathy Ketcham, for mentorship and friendship

Jason Schwartz at Dawn Farm, for sharing resources

Michael V. Genovese, M.D., J.D., ABIHM, for kindly reviewing
this work from a scientific perspective

Janice, Tom, and Danielle, for teaching me the basics

Petra Fallaux and Ginger, Jeff Oaks and Andy, for the walks and talks

George and Justin, for the playlists

Darlene, Suz Falvey, and Jim, for the workouts

Erika Freiberger, for skilled bodywork

Christina Sible at Yoga on Centre, for yoga instruction

Susan Piver, for meditation instruction

Pittsburgh Friends Meeting and Pittsburgh Shambhala Center,
for silence

Nick, for perseverance through all the years and for our son

Grateful acknowledgment is made to Scott Gonzalez, M.D., and
Opiate Detox Recovery (www.heroin-detox.com) for permission to
reprint passages that originally appeared on that site.

Some names of people quoted in this work have been changed
to preserve anonymity, but all the stories told here are true.
I have tried my best to represent these stories faithfully.
Any errors of fact are mine.

The
RECOVERING
BODY

Introduction
Come Home

. . . .

The day I was asked to write this book I had just finished talking about addiction and recovery with a bunch of medical students from across the country. I was standing on the sidewalk of a crowded downtown street, looking at my phone, checking my email, and the editor who sent the message asked me whether I'd consider writing a book about "exercise and recovery." I laughed out loud, because as an immediate response to this question, my mind had cued up and rerun a grainy but vivid home video of the "bike-hike" my sixth-grade class held almost forty years before to raise money for our overnight class trip to Gettysburg.

This home movie is stored in my mind's archives as Exhibit A in the trials of my "fat, ugly body" and its consistently lousy performance in moments of stress, pleasure, even ordinary days. ("Fat" and "ugly"—these are the words the offscreen narrator uses about the movie's subject: me. Of course, in my addictive mind, It's Always About Me.) Once the movie is cued up, I'm forced to watch as the footage unwinds. One warm spring Saturday, we all brought our bikes to school with the purpose of riding one hundred laps around the paved lot between the school and the church next door, a distance calculated to be ten miles. When we were done, we'd go back to our sponsors and collect pledges for each mile we'd ridden.

Ten miles on a bike seemed like a trip to the moon for me at eleven years old. I had a bike, all right: a pink girls' bike with a white vinyl banana-seat and swoop handlebars, a bit small for my body since my dad had given it to me when I was seven. But because we lived deep in the suburbs, with no sidewalks and no roads safe for bikes, I never rode the damn thing. Hell, I never even walked anywhere. We lived between two farms, so we had no neighbors and no "neighborhood." Our house was surrounded by woods, and my mother—who was raising her three kids on the Long Shelf Life diet (Twinkies, Wonder Bread, Lucky Charms, Coke)—didn't let us wander past the pear tree at the back of the yard. If she could have chained or microchipped us, she might have, but as it was, she didn't trust us to roam. It seems to me now that I was a bit like a feedlot animal being fattened up for the slaughter. And as in the film *Groundhog Day*, that small death happened over and over again when the kids at school teased me about the shape of my body and its inability to perform in gym class. So when the bike-hike rolled around, I made it maybe five or six miles. I was reduced to asking two of the boys—Brian and Doug, who were stringy and fit from Little League training and had finished way ahead of me—to make up my distance.

I was the one who was picked last for every team. I was the one who fell off the monkey bars, who couldn't hold the flexed-arm hang in the Presidential Fitness Test. Faith Ann, who grew up not far from me on a real farm, rode horses, and took care of the animals, could pull her chin over the bar.

The salty playground sweat was corrosive on my lips, and even today the memory of its taste lingers in my mouth, mixed with dust. When I got home, to dull the pain of shame, I reached for the Ho Hos snack cakes.

Me, write a book about fitness?

Absolutely. Because this is also a book about recovery. About our capacity to change once we quit numbing out with any substance—heroin, booze, methamphetamine, Xanax, sugar, nicotine, anything—and start healing.

After a quick rerun of my *Ride of Shame* home movie, I stood in the street and fired off an email to my friend Patrick, fifty-five, an athlete and a writer. In his early forties Patrick quit running marathons to save his knees; he now competes in triathlons. He also has more than thirty years sober. In response to my email, Patrick said he thought physical recovery was an undercovered subject that deserved more consideration. "Imagine a meeting whose topic is physical fitness," he said. "It's almost unthinkable." Yet, he said, recovery of the body is so much a part of healing for so many of us—perhaps more important and central to our lives than any particular Step among the Twelve that many of us take.

But Twelve Step programs alone don't do the job. Or rather, when I am as rigorously honest as my system of recovery asks me to be, I have to admit that my body needs as much care as my spirit. Addiction is at least as much a physical illness as a spiritual one. When we call it an illness, however, most people are wont to think of the solution in terms of standard Western medical remedies: drugs and devices. The medical community has become so reliant on these "fixes" for illness that the choice many of us make to live as drug-free as possible constitutes a New Counterculture. "That's a great statement—I really like that," says Kevin McCauley, M.D., a former Marine pilot and flight surgeon, now medical director for a couple of Utah treatment facilities. He has eight years sober from prescription painkillers. "It's opting out of the typical paradigm of consumerism. When a person says, 'I'm not going to use drugs, and I'm not going to accept these highly marketed pharmaceuticals either,' then he or she is saying, 'I'm going to reassess everything.'"

Part of that reassessment is physical recovery, which, in general, makes up too small a part of the care plans of U.S. treatment facilities. Many people in recovery have found not just relief but, as McCauley mentions, an entire paradigm shift, simply through learning to take care of their bodies.

I told the editor I'd do it. And almost immediately, I had a couple of "Big Bang" insights that showed me how important this subject is for people in recovery.

On a hot Friday in July, I drove to New York City. Into the back of my car I'd loaded the road bike I'd bought three months earlier. There's no more intimate way to see a city than by bike, and the next morning I rode the Hudson River Greenway from 9th Street to 125th Street, where I veered east and climbed the hill to the Columbia University campus, then down to Morningside Heights—an easy fifteen miles. It was partly sunny, 85 degrees, and the sweat flew off my face. I met up with Patrick on the Upper West Side, and we went to an afternoon meeting. Then in the evening he took me along for his favorite New York City ride: Central Park after dark. We slipped through the tall iron gates at 110th Street and rode counterclockwise with the traffic. Patrick lives in New York City, doesn't own a car, and doesn't often take cabs. He uses his bike to commute throughout the city, and he showed me how to negotiate the traffic. I asked whether he used bike lanes, and he laughed outright. Of course his body is much stronger than mine: he was training for the Chicago triathlon. Even on his heavy steel hybrid bike he sped ahead of me on the uphill stretches, and I'd catch up to him on the downhill. We rode one-and-a-half circuits—nine miles—around the lamp-lit park, keeping an eye out for raccoons. Then I followed him as he merged onto Fifth Avenue near the Plaza Hotel. I was staying in Great Jones Street in the NoHo neighborhood.

"I'll ride with you back downtown," he said.

At ten o'clock on a Saturday night in high summer, in prime club-hopping time, we flew down the three-mile stretch of Fifth Avenue from Central Park to Washington Square.

Fifth Avenue is not made for cyclists. Yellow cabs darted back and forth around us like swarms of hornets.

I could feel my mind flipping out with anxiety, telling myself all kinds of stories about how stupid we were, but my body saved me: I'd already ridden twenty-five miles *(twenty-five miles!)* that day through Manhattan traffic, and the more I thought about that number, the more I realized I could trust my body. As I let go of the freak-out story my mind was writing, I felt my body relax into following this person whose skill I trusted. At one point I nearly got popped by two cabs fighting for a spot at the curb, but my body's split-second responses came to my rescue. In that instant I understood that a cab could take either one of us out for good. Yet paradoxically there we were, haring south between the glittering walls of Fifth Avenue's neon-draped skyscrapers on a starlit Saturday night, completely present and aware, telling each other stories at red lights, choosing to do something healthy with our bodies rather than drinking and partying and spending tons of cash. Of course there's no language that's not cliché to describe the gestalt of the scene: "Center of the universe"? "Heart of civilization"? *The core of the Big Apple?*

My mind kept wailing, *Holy shit, we're out of our fucking minds!*

But my body powering my bike and pumping out a steady bass line brought me back to awareness of the import of what I was doing at that moment. Because, after all, the body lives only in the present. The mind can wallow in the past or future-trip out the wazoo, but the body is right here, right now.

My mother's face rose in my mind's eye. At age fifty-eight—just four years older than my friend Patrick was then—she died of lung cancer from a lifetime of chain-smoking. She had suffered an abusive childhood at the hands of a violent alcoholic father—much more damaging than my childhood—an experience from which she never recovered. As Patrick and I soared toward the arch in Washington Square, "Big Bang" Insight #1 exploded: the feeling washed over me that I was doing something she had never done in her life. She had lived and died and never recovered from this disease, never enjoyed this kind of release and pleasure and feeling of health and freedom.

But there was more. The next day, I drove through Queens and out Long Island toward Islip and stepped onto a ferry to Fire Island.

I'd left my car and my bike on the mainland. I carried just a few necessities. A close friend—a woman who's like a big sister to me in recovery—who takes a house on Fire Island every summer was coming to meet me at the dock. The thirty-mile bike ride had relaxed and opened up my body so much that I could breathe practically down to my toes. I could smell the sea, feel the salt air on my skin, hear the water and wildlife in acute ways that are impossible when I spend my days closed up, working in tunnel-vision before a computer screen. My body was hungry and pleasantly tired. As I sat on the ferry's top deck watching the sun set and the fog roll in as the boat glided across the sound, I felt enormous joy bloom inside my chest, at first slowly like rising bread dough, then like bursting white light, as though my ribs would rip apart.

At the same time as my body felt that joy, my mind closed in, saying, *You do not get to feel this.*

"Big Bang" Insight #2: my illness wants to separate me from my body.

My mind is afraid of sharp edges, and as the poet David Whyte says, joy carries just as sharp an edge as sorrow. So in an effort to protect me from loss, my mind enacts this divide—it distorts the truth, and distortion of truth is a sentinel feature of addiction. Because I practice meditation—not well, not every day, not for long, but I do it—I've learned to recognize this divide as a moment at which I have a choice about whether to enact self-compassion or self-hatred.

You do not get to feel this, my mind insisted.

Self-hatred.

But if I'm going to heal, I have to live inside my skin and bones. I sat on the deck and brought my attention back to the salt air moving into my lungs, and I felt myself sink back into my body. When I came back to my body, I could allow myself to feel that joy. I could talk back to my mind: *I'm feeling joy. It's real. It's the truth.*

Self-compassion.

Recovery keeps teaching me that when I'm confused about what's true, I have the option of coming back home to my body—it will tell me the truth.

They say in recovery that we're moving either toward a drink or drug, or away from a drink or drug. I used to think that with enough "time," I'd finally get to the place where the drink or drug would be lost on the horizon, and I could just sit back and coast a bit. But the small time I have (four-and-a-half years, as of this writing) is teaching me that I never stop moving, and that sobriety is a state that I move into and out of—and back into—all the time. It's like the color spectrum: I'm sometimes on fire and closer to red; other times I've cooled off and I'm closer to blue.

How do we know which direction we're moving? How do we know what the colors mean? One way is to come home to the truth of the body. This book is about the wisdom, self-compassion, and healing we find when we move back into the body as our first and last home—and about the active addiction that takes over when we abandon our bodies like condemned houses. Because that's what addiction is: self-abandonment.

While I was writing this book, I had a chance to sit down with Don Miguel Ruiz, author of the book *The Four Agreements,* and his son, Don Miguel Ruiz Jr., author of *The Five Levels of Attachment.* The elder Don Miguel, himself a physician, suffered a massive heart attack in 2002 and eight years later underwent a heart transplant. During that eight-year interim, his heart was functioning at 16 percent capacity. Essentially he was forced to carry his sick body around, waiting for an opportunity to recover—the way I had felt when I was detoxing. I ask them how Don Miguel managed to function for eight years with so little heart capacity. Didn't he feel as though his body had betrayed him and refused to do what he wanted it to do? Wasn't he frustrated and angry? I am thinking about the way I sometimes feel when my distorted thinking takes over and tells me, *You don't get to feel/do/have this.* I pick up stakes and move out of my body, and when I do that, I feel as though I'm forced to carry around a bag of rocks. I feel depleted of energy—frustrated and angry—and I want to drink or use to get rid of that feeling.

"The body will follow whatever command he sends," Don Miguel Jr. says. "Even if it's sick with a 102- or 103-degree fever, if I push my body, it'll try its best to do my will. Which means even when it's sick, the body is loyal to us. But the problem is, we don't accept the truth that it's sick. Which means we're not going to take care of it. And instead of accepting the truth and taking care of it, we're punishing it for what it is: 'How dare you betray me?' We're not even taking care of the truth that the body needs healing."

Taking care of the truth: an elegant way to rephrase the idea of "rigorous honesty," I thought. But when we're caught inside the distortions of addictive thinking, how can we know what the truth is?

"My dad accepted the truth of his heart condition," explains Don Miguel Jr. "He decided, 'I'm going to be patient with my body. I'm going to push it, but I'm also going to be tender. I'm going to be careful. I'm not going to give it what it doesn't need.' For example, if his body doesn't need salt—because salt will make him sick—he doesn't take salt for ten years."

Taking care of the truth: if my body doesn't need alcohol or drugs because they'll make me sick, I don't take alcohol or drugs.

But what if the body isn't really telling you the truth? my inward skeptic insists.

You do not get to feel this.

"I watched your Oprah interview," I tell Don Miguel. "She asked you where you felt most at home, and you said, 'In my body.' Do you think the body lies?"

"The body?" he says. "No. Not the body. The *mind* lies."

The body and mind have to work and play in concert each day. It may be the mind that lies, the mind that tells the body, "We need a shot and a beer," but it is the body that pours the drink into the glass and down the throat.

So along with exploring the physical fitness required to train the body to work with the mind, this book also explores the mental and spiritual fitness required to train the mind to work with the body. To take care of its truths, help it recover, and avoid forcing it to do what will hurt it.

Taking care of my body is a large part of the work I've learned to do to stay sober. And yet only once have I heard the body brought up as a topic at a meeting: a newcomer wanted to talk about sexuality, and she wisely raised the subject at a women's meeting. The result was a round of deep storytelling about the body's truths that the women who attended that meeting still remember. That's how rare it is to talk about the recovering body in meetings: "Remember that One Epic Meeting we had—years ago—about sex?" We'll talk about any spiritual principle, but broach the subject of the body, and we find out how fast people can scramble for donuts, coffee, a cigarette, or a bathroom break.

Ignoring the body, however, is participating in denial. Because where do we live all day? In our bodies.

So in the following chapters I will explore, first, the ways drugs trash the home where we live, and then five practices to clean up the wreckage and recover the body's health: exercise, nutrition, sleep and rest, sexuality and pleasure, and meditation and awareness. Each chapter's practice is backed up by scientific research, as well as the experiences of people in long-term recovery. I've talked with national and international experts here, but in gathering examples of people who are recovering their bodies I've reached out to folks close to home who have adopted simple practices that don't cost an arm and a leg. You don't need to hire experts or personal chefs or spend a fortune on a gym membership. You can start with the people in your own community. You can try this at home.

I've always used the word "sober" to describe myself in recovery. But what does "sober" really mean? It's not just about staying away from booze. (Booze wasn't even my thing in the main part of my addiction.) The word comes from the Latin word "sobrius," which has two parts. The second part, the Latin suffix "–brius," means "not-drunk," or "not-filled-up" (the opposite of "–ebrius," from which we get "inebriated," "drunk," "filled-up"). Then there's the ancient Indo-European root prefix "so-," which has connotations of the collective self: "ourselves" and "we." My friend Jenn Ferris-Glick, who works in a neuroscience lab, teaches yoga, and has six years sober, and whom you will meet in these pages, calls this the "capital-S Self." The Self that is not enslaved by ego.

So we can think of being "sober" as being filled-up with the capital-S Self. As moving back into the house, Coming Home. Moving and making a home takes hard work, discipline, and a supportive community.

A lot of folks without addiction achieve this Self connection by staying in touch with their community of "we," their extended families and friends. Those of us whose families have been fractured by addiction have to put together our own supportive communities. In my experience there's nothing more healing than love. If I believe in any higher powers, then real love, unselfish love, is certainly one of them. (I'll mention some others later.)

I detoxed in November 2008—but just because my body was "clean" doesn't mean I was sober. It took me more than a year of living without drugs, and then a relapse, to begin to do my recovery in a way that helped me heal. Just being drug-free wasn't enough. I had to let people love me, and then more recently I've had to learn how to love myself. Love ain't always about good times; love often requires us to do stuff we don't feel like doing. It's not fun separating ourselves from friends who continue to use, learning how to eat good food, kicking our butts out the door to exercise instead of lying in bed all morning—or forgiving ourselves for eating potato chips in our pajamas all day and gently allowing ourselves to start again. But when I manage this, I find out that love and compassion are always more reliable incentives than punishment. Love is always more transformational than coercion. When I can take care of this body—the house in which I live—with love instead of force, I have a chance at discovering who I am and what I'm made of. I give myself a chance to grow.

This book is partly the story of how I—and many others I know—move out and then back into more or less sober states of mind, by moving out (even just one foot out, or one toe out) of our bodies, and then moving back in. If your house needs some rehab, or if you know someone with addiction and want to support that person in healing, I hope you'll find some practices and stories here that will set you on your way toward recovering the body—that may enable you to come back and live in peace in the home that is your birthright.

Slumdogging
Ways Addiction Trashes the Body

Anger's my meat; I sup upon myself,
And so shall starve with feeding.

—William Shakespeare, *Coriolanus,* act 4, scene 2

Let me draw you a picture of what addiction can do to the body. I have some photos of a woman I know that were made just before she started detoxing from several years of addiction to high levels of prescription painkillers. When I say "high levels," I don't mean three or four or even ten Vicodin per day. I mean two years of taking, each day, 150 milligrams of pure hydrocodone, plus 120 milligrams of morphine, plus fentanyl lollipops. How much heroin would that equal? It's hard to tell. Heroin purity varies; dime bags are said to contain roughly 100 milligrams of powder, 15 to 30 percent of which might be the drug. So she was using the equivalent of at least a dozen and possibly as many as three dozen dime bags per day.

Unlike heroin, pharmaceutical drugs are guaranteed pure by the manufacturer and the U.S. Food and Drug Administration (FDA). At the time the photo was shot, her doctor was prescribing a 100-microgram fentanyl skin patch every two days. Fentanyl is a powerful opioid that's sometimes cut into heroin, bagged, and stamped with names like "Overdose" and "Suicide." Early in 2014, just before Philip Seymour Hoffman fatally overdosed, heroin laced with fentanyl and stamped "Theraflu" killed more than eighty people in the United States, including twenty-two in southwestern Pennsylvania, twenty-five in Rhode Island, and at least thirty-seven in Maryland. Estimates vary as to exactly how strong fentanyl is when absorbed through the skin, partly because each person's body absorbs it at different rates, and partly because the experts, the "geniuses" who invented fentanyl and those who prescribe it, simply don't know. Morphine is the gold standard to which the strength of all opiates is compared, and according to most extant data, this woman was being prescribed the equivalent of 400 to 500 milligrams of oral morphine per day. And since she was in active addiction, she was, of course, taking more than that.

"Four hundred or five hundred milligrams of morphine—I don't know how much that is," some people say when I tell them this story. Here are a couple of ways to think about her level of drug use. When my mother was dying of lung cancer that had invaded her spinal cord and brain, her doctor prescribed 40 milligrams of morphine twice a day. When my father was dying of gastrointestinal cancer that had eaten through his guts and lungs and had fractured the humerus bone in his upper left arm— damage that cast him into extreme pain—he was given one-quarter the amount of fentanyl this woman had been prescribed. So she was on a serious shitload of drugs.

The first thing I notice is that she is thin. Her collarbones and cheekbones are sticking out. The veins on the back of her hands, the cords in her neck, the tendons on the backs of her fingers are sticking out. She reminds me of a praying mantis. Most sources cite normal body mass index for women as a range from 18.5 to 24.9, and this woman was at the bottom of that range.

Her skin is pale. She's wearing makeup, but it looks as though it's applied to a plaster model.

According to records made at the time, other things were going wrong with this woman's body, even apart from the two neurological disorders for which she was being prescribed these drugs. For example, from the start of her course on morphine, she went into menopause and stayed there until the morphine was replaced with another drug two years later. Because the drugs disabled her ovaries, she lost enough bone mass to make her doctor consider giving her yet other drugs to treat osteoporosis. Her sleep cycles and appetites had become dysfunctional. All these problems can be caused by high levels of painkillers, but you'd never have known that from the way her doctor kept bumping up her doses.

If you had passed this woman on the street, you may not have been able to tell there was anything wrong with her. She didn't look like "a junkie." In the photo her hair is clean and styled; her T-shirt is old, but it's tucked into dark-wash skinny designer jeans. Her teeth are all white and all there.

As I study the photo, I keep coming back to her gauntness. She was five feet, five inches, and weighed about 113 pounds. This woman actually considered her scrawniness one of the benefits of taking painkillers: in white Western post-industrial culture, skinny-ass women are thought of as super-hot. (At least we women are told they are.) She never felt like eating. All opioids slow the gut and suppress appetites; "heroin-chic" was a term coined to describe the emaciated "beauty" of runway models who had become addicted to dope. Childlike in their appearance, "waif" was another term the culture gave them. When it was coined in the Victorian era, the word "waif" referred to a homeless child, a starving "street urchin."

The woman in the photo behaved like a child, all right. Most of the time, she wasn't taking control of her life. Obviously she wasn't feeding herself well. And her addiction had made her homeless. By "homeless" I don't mean she was living under a bridge (like "a junkie"). She had a nice house in a middle-class part of town. But if you think of the body as the place where we live all day, this woman had lost her ability to reside there. She stopped by occasionally to cut the grass and check the heating and plumbing, but the shades were drawn. Nobody was living there.

Another photo I have of this woman has always stuck in my mind, a shot taken a few months before the other. In it, she's lying on her bed next to her little boy. Her son's face is round and healthy, his lips rosy, his dark eyes flashing as he smiles at the camera. Her face, free of makeup in this photo, is colorless. By "colorless" I mean quite literally without color.

Her pallor is almost gray, except for the skin around her eyes, which is sepia, as though she hasn't slept well for nights on end. And her body looks drained of life.

Yeah, that was me, the woman in the pictures.

My body could have suffered much more damage if, instead of taking painkillers, I had been drinking. In terms of sheer abuse to the body, booze beats dope, crack, and meth hands down. The British medical journal *The Lancet* made front-page news worldwide a few years back when it ranked alcohol as a Class A dangerous drug, along with the others I just listed. Alcohol was judged 25 percent more harmful than heroin, the next most dangerous drug. The researchers scored the drugs (which, it seems, did not include prescription painkillers) according to sixteen criteria regarding each drug's harms, with drug-specific and drug-related death and illness at the top of the list, followed by dependence and impairment of mental functioning. All of these are ways that drugs trash the body.

In public-health terms, it's very hard to conceive of the sheer scale of physical damage addiction does. It's even hard to do by cropping the picture to just alcoholism in the United States. Nobody ever has been able to calculate the number of U.S. alcoholics, but the Centers for Disease Control and Prevention (CDC) estimate that 17.6 million people "abuse" or are "dependent" on alcohol and that another several million binge drink. Alcoholism and "heavy drinking" cause a major portion of the total U.S. social and economic burden of illness. It's estimated that on any given day about 40 percent of U.S. hospital beds are occupied by people suffering health problems resulting from alcohol abuse. More than half of all U.S. adults have alcoholism running in their families, and more than seven million American kids are growing up with active alcoholism in the household.

Teenage drinking is the way addiction starts for many—including my father, grandfather, and cousin, all of whom died of the consequences of addiction. And drug use can screw up, sometimes permanently, normal adolescent development. They may look a lot like adults, but adolescents are much more vulnerable to the effects of alcohol—especially their brains, central nervous systems, and endocrine systems—because they're still growing.

In Gabor Maté's extraordinary, award-winning book *In the Realm of Hungry Ghosts: Close Encounters with Addiction* about heroin addiction in Vancouver, British Columbia, the Canadian physician makes clear the ways this physical (and emotional) devastation spreads like a wake in the generations that come after each person who remains untreated. Maté is one of the few addiction experts who draws sustained attention in his writing and lectures to the results of the CDC's Adverse Childhood Experiences (ACE) Study, a long-term study of more than 17,000 participants that shows addiction is one of many illnesses that result from unhealed damage in childhood. These adverse experiences include suffering physical, verbal, and emotional abuse or neglect; living with parents who have untreated addiction or mental illness; witnessing abuse of a parent; and living at home while a parent is in prison. These stresses, Maté says, can express or "switch on" the genes that make a kid susceptible to addiction. The ACE study shows conclusively that the more adverse childhood experiences, the more likely the adverse outcomes. If a child sustains more than one or two adverse experiences and begins using drugs to manage the resultant stress before the age of twenty-one, he says, addiction is extremely likely to result.

Despite what some strains of medical investigation and public opinion would have us believe, many people with addiction can achieve abstinent recovery from the worst low-bottom situations. But spiritual recovery and physical recovery are two different propositions. There may be no "ceiling" on spiritual recovery—emotionally, the sky may be the limit on healing—but if we do enough lasting physical damage, recovering our bodies may be a harder row to hoe. Still, with enough education and practice, we can recover more fully than we often think. For example, I have a friend who began drinking as a teenager and, despite chronic asthma, progressed to smoking crack. She now has more than four years clean, and she holds down a job, goes to school, and takes care of all five of her daughters. Many people would think that in itself is a miracle— and it is, but it's not the end goal of her recovery. Part of her work now is cultivating willingness to confront the truth about the damage she did to her lungs by smoking crack and cigarettes. She spent the past winter—a hard one—with recurrent bronchitis, which several times came close to descending into pneumonia. I've only used pharma drugs and booze, so I ask her, "Is smoking crack that bad for your lungs?" and immediately I feel like a naïve freak, but she doesn't treat me that way.

It's not the extreme heat of the pipe, she tells me. "It's the impurities in the crack," she says. Just as you never know what shit your heroin is cut with, you never know what compounds the DIY chemist used to cook up the rocks.

"That," she says, "and the copper Chore Boy scrubber you use to filter the damn stuff. You suck enough of that shit down and it's gonna wreck your lungs." She now smokes just two cigarettes per day, and she's determined to quit those.

There are other ways addiction trashes the body that you may not have thought about.

Much of addiction's physical damage starts with assaults to the brain and central nervous system. Most of the rest of the damage cascades down from there, because the finely tuned actions in various regions of the brain govern the body's other systems. The one big exception is the liver, which takes its own direct hits in working tirelessly to detoxify our bodies and, in active addiction, never being able to catch up.

Most people know alcoholic withdrawal can result in hallucinations and life-threatening seizures. It's also common knowledge that alcoholism can cause several kinds of brain damage, including dementia, stroke, and "wet brain" or Wernicke-Korsakoff syndrome. Booze also sedates the body, and when we can't wake up, our bodies crave some kind of stimulant. So maybe we look for speed. Amphetamines further screw with sleep cycles, resulting in irritability and insomnia. This goes for prescription amphetamines—the attention deficit/hyperactivity disorder (ADHD) meds Ritalin and Adderall. Many people think of Adderall as coffee in a pill. My university undergrads tell me stories about using Adderall to improve concentration on tests and to pull all-nighters, whether to study or to party. "Where can you get this stuff?" I once asked a classroom full of eighteen-year-olds. There was silence as their eyes shifted around at each other.

"Anywhere," one said.

"In the library," another said.

"In the *library?* You can buy Adderall in the university library?" I demanded, full-throttle mom voice kicking in. My kid is just two years younger than they are. "*Where* in the library?"

They shrugged. "Anywhere," one girl said.

The human body is not built to process the constant dopamine deluges caused by chronic amphetamine use. In high doses over time, speed makes *Homo sapiens* into "tweakers": restless, manic, euphoric, grandiose. On meth or cocaine the brain may hallucinate and create paranoid delusions, say, of ants crawling under the skin, so we scratch and scratch. The body may refuse food and sleep—as in, tweakers may starve and stay awake for a week straight. Speed and coke also tell the brain to squeeze the heart's major arteries, and blood pressure will skyrocket. The arteries just aren't designed for this kind of radical, chronic elasticity, so methamphetamine and cocaine use are strongly linked with coronary artery disease and stroke. When the body finally crashes and then wakes up, it will crave more speed to dig its way out of its crater of depression.

A few borrowed bars of a benzodiazepine (benzo), we think—a few Xanax or Valium—will take care of our sleep problems. The longer I'm sober, the more I thank my lucky stars that I never messed around with benzos. I know adults who as children were diagnosed with panic attacks and "generalized anxiety disorder" and were started on short courses of benzos. Those short courses slowly morphed into longer courses and then into a lifetime on drugs. After fifteen or twenty years, some of them are still trying to quit.

Although the positive powers of pharmaceutical drugs ought to be respected—painkillers, after all, *do* kill some kinds of pain; benzodiazepines *can* help with panic attacks in the short-term, as in less than two weeks—benzos are frightening in their tenacity about changing the body's ability to adapt to stress. Among the most damaging of their harmful effects when taken long-term are an increase in the anxiety they're designed to treat, depression, aggression, impaired ability to think, memory problems, personality changes, and mood swings. All these side effects can lead to deterioration in relationships, which leads to more fragmented sleep and increases in dosages. And the snowball picks up speed. Long-term benzo use is also linked with degeneration of sleep architecture—less deep sleep or outright insomnia—and exacerbation of sleep apnea. And anyone who drinks at the same time as they're taking benzos risks fatal overdose.

Most people, even those without addiction, trying to detox from long-term benzo use find that it takes months, if not years, for them to recover from a host of problems: headaches; insomnia and fatigue, and concomitant restlessness; muscle weakness, pain, spasms, and tremors; blood-pressure changes; nausea and weight loss; and light and sound sensitivity. I mean, what a list. Such torturous physical discomfort can seriously challenge anyone's willingness to recover.

Similarly, painkillers damage a person's general quality of life by numbing the brain and central nervous system. So if we're lucky enough not to overdose by respiratory depression, we spend our hazy daze of painkiller addiction in a half-life of numbness. Like alcohol, painkillers sedate the body's neurology and make it uncoordinated. It's not just that we've suddenly become lazy: because we're sedated or no longer sure of our balance or endurance, we may not get enough exercise.

Addiction's assaults on the brain also affect the endocrine system, which governs our sex lives and metabolisms—our bodies' ability to feel hungry for food, exercise, beauty, sleep, pleasure. Opioids, alcohol, and benzos all inhibit sex-hormone production, which can lead to premature ejaculation, low sexual desire, and erectile dysfunction (ED). So we go to the doctor with ED that's treated with Viagra, but the underlying cause—addiction—is usually ignored. Teenage boys who drink and experience even short-term low testosterone set themselves up for a greater risk of experiencing it later. For heavy-drinking men, sexual problems are common, and the men are likely to deal with the resultant relationship problems by drinking more. As for girls, teens who drink run the risk of disrupting a normal start of puberty and inhibiting their growth and bone health—which can happen even when girls aren't drinking enough to damage their liver or other organs.

Not too many people who start taking painkillers or shooting heroin understand that they're seriously screwing with their sex lives. Opioids numb out the hypothalamus, the part of the midbrain that controls the glands that govern the sex organs. Opioid addiction, like alcoholism, can also inhibit the production of estrogen and testosterone. This is why the doctor wanted to put me on drugs for osteoporosis: estrogen protects against bone loss, and in early opioid-induced menopause, my bone density was draining away.

The opposite happens with amphetamines' and cocaine's effects on sexuality—people often become compulsively sexual. But meth and coke, especially crack, will increase the body's energy and lower the mind's inhibitions so much that people who use these drugs report engaging in sex that's much riskier than usual, so they're more likely to contract the HIV virus/AIDS, hepatitis, and other infections.

The immune system is an exquisitely responsive physical organization. Within seconds, the smallest paper cut triggers a global response in the body, advancing clotting mechanisms, infection-fighting substances, and pain control. With stimulant use, these high-speed rails of the immune response will be blocked or broken. Colds will take longer to pass, sores will take longer to heal, skin will break out in uncontrollable acne that meth users especially pick at compulsively in their restlessness. It has been documented that meth users' faces can age twenty years in the space of a few months. If you think this is an exaggeration, visit the *Faces of Meth* online (www.facesofmeth.us/main.htm) and you will see ordinary people whose addictions to speed rendered them unrecognizable.

When it comes to fighting infection, addiction lowers our resistance by killing off the rainforest of bacteria that under normal conditions live in our gut. More than half our immune system comes from the climate these flora promote, and alcohol is especially toxic to their health. Most alcoholics live with conditions such as hemorrhoids, chronic flatulence, constipation, and diarrhea. When the gut isn't healthy, a virus that ought to pass quickly can linger for weeks or months and turn into bronchitis or pneumonia.

And then there's the liver. In recovery I have become especially fond of my liver. I try to look after it, and this is no joke. The word "liver," as you might suspect, comes directly from the word "life." In Old English, the word for the organ was "lifer," and the fact is that without a healthy liver the body cannot survive.

The liver's work is critical to almost every other organ in the body. The liver makes amino acids and cholesterol. It stores energy for the body and is the queen of metabolism. We think of the liver as a "filter," but it actually converts toxic substances that could poison the body by accumulating in body fat into water-soluble chemicals that can be ferried to the bladder and disposed of in the bathroom. So I think of the liver more as a washing machine than as a filter. Overloading the washing machine—using drugs—prevents it from doing its job efficiently.

You can find your liver under the right bottom edge of your ribs: if you poke around in there and feel hardness or pain, you had better get to a doctor.

Have you ever seen a drinker who's thin everywhere except for his big beer gut? This is probably a sign that his liver is failing. Heavy drinking can damage the liver by causing fatty liver, alcoholic hepatitis, liver cancer, and finally that grande dame of alcoholism, cirrhosis. In cirrhosis, the liver cells thicken and become hard with scar tissue.

In 2012, alcoholic cirrhosis was the twelfth leading cause of death in the United States. In 2007, it killed almost 30,000 Americans. Add that to all the other causes of death secondary to untreated addiction to substances—all the cancers, the lung diseases, type 2 diabetes, as well as fatal overdoses, accidents, homicides—and addiction is perhaps the primary killer of bodies in our society.

Like most people with addiction, I never thought I'd be able to live drug-free. Come to that, many Americans without addiction don't think they can live drug-free. More than half of us are on at least two medications, and at least one out of four women my age are taking an antidepressant—which is one of the top three classes of prescription drugs Americans take. The other two are antibiotics and, you guessed it, opioid painkillers.

After I finally did detox over the course of two months in late 2008, the post-acute withdrawal syndrome (PAWS) made me seriously reconsider, every day, whether I could actually live drug-free. That's what I wanted: to live drug-free. I wanted to believe I didn't need to take drugs every day just to live. But with PAWS I had mood swings and headaches. I couldn't drag my ass out of bed. My body suffered cold flashes, as though an icy wave had crashed over me. For weeks my legs kicked, I sneezed, and my eyes watered.

Worst of all, I couldn't sleep.

"Just suck it up," I was told by people with years of clean-and-sober time. "Nobody ever died from lack of sleep."

Bullshit, I thought. *I'm gonna die if I don't get some sleep.* In fact, if you've got fibromyalgia (I do), you have to get regular sleep or you can throw yourself into a pain flare that lasts weeks and compromises your sobriety. (For weeks I kept a script for fentanyl in my purse. Just in case.) In fact, if you're just a normal person who wants to go to work and raise her kids and pay the bills, you need good sleep. In fact, preventing sleep is on Amnesty International's list of torture methods.

"Pray," I was told.

"Nobody can keep you sober," I was told. "Remember: 'no human power.'"

Praying is cool—I'll show you why later in this book—but it doesn't do much when your body is kicking and sweating and weeping involuntarily, when it can neither exercise nor sleep. I prayed, and I worked some of the Twelve Steps—nine of them, twice—and I put together about a year of time before the suffering in my neglected body got to be too much, and I relapsed.

I stole a Vicodin. My very favorite beloved awesomest drug on the face of the planet. I stole two, I ate one, and I put the other one back.

"Give yourself a limited amount of time to beat yourself up," my sponsor said the next day. "Then get on with the work."

The work. I knew I'd have to do something different this time. If I were going to be absolutely honest, I'd have to pay attention to my body's recovery. I couldn't focus solely on mental, emotional, spiritual fitness. I had to tell the truth: I was living in a house called "My Body," and I had done it some serious damage.

But how to go about recovering it?

Moving the Body
Recovery and Exercise

· ·

It is often said that exercise is medicine,
but a more correct statement is that insufficient
regular exercise is abnormal and pathological.

–Daniel E. Lieberman, professor of human evolutionary
biology at Harvard University and author of *The Story of the
Human Body: Evolution, Health, and Disease*

When I was twenty-four, after working a couple years as a newspaper
reporter I went back to school for a master's degree in writing. I'd spent
several thousand hours in newsrooms reading Associated Press wire
copy written at an eighth-grade reading level, so it took me a while to
get used to reading French linguistics theorists. But I made a running
start on writing my first book manuscript and learned how to maintain
authority in a classroom with students who were only five or six years
younger than I was. And I ended the academic year totally stressed out.
I'd broken off an eighteen-month relationship with a heavy-drinking
and physically mean guy, had a fling with another heavy drinker, and
fell for yet a third one (see any patterns?) who was sleeping with someone else.

I counted myself lucky when, before summer break arrived, I snagged an off-the-books job waiting tables. One weekend, I came back after my shift to find the apartment I shared with a friend ransacked, with several of her valuables missing.

I lost my ability to cope. Intellectually I was ahead of my years, but emotionally I was twenty-four going on about fourteen. When my room-mate moved out and left me hanging with the lease, I did what I had to do—I told my landlord I wanted to leave, negotiated for my security deposit, put it down on a new apartment, and moved. But the way I man-aged my feelings was to reenact what I'd learned in my original family. I refused to admit I had any feelings about any of this, and then I drank and binged on cookies and other sweet stuff.

Rationalizing that I was "staying cool" that summer of 1989, I'd mix myself frozen drinks with pricey, gut-wrenching ingredients like Kahlua liqueur or peach schnapps—each one loaded with sugar. I'd scarf down entire bags of Chips Ahoy and Pepperidge Farm Milano cookies. I ate alone, and because that felt so lonely and loser-ish, I drank alone. ("One of my biggest triggers throughout my entire life is feeling lonely," says my friend Nicole, thirty-four, a personal trainer and gym manager with nine years sober.) I gained twenty-five or thirty pounds within a couple of months, so much weight so fast that my hips and breasts still bear the web of silver stretch marks from those binges. I didn't even have stretch marks after carrying my son—so those are the only stretch marks of my life.

Toward the end of the academic year, I sat in one of my seminars and doodled a list of things I wanted to do that summer. I found this list the other day in a notebook at the bottom of a box, like a time capsule from another life. The list's top items (this is for real):

Buy a bicycle
Get drunk
Eat chocolate
Sew a black linen dress

This is Jen In Graduate School, Making Plans.

As you can see, except for the bike, I'd packed up and moved out of my body. And when it came to the bike, here was my strategy: I would buy a bike, then go home, get wasted, and eat a load of chocolate. I wanted a bike, but in those days I didn't believe I could have what I wanted, so I drank and used.

The desire to ride a bike is not a theory—it's a sensation you feel inside your body: you want to put your body on the machine and move. Preferably fast. But feeling the emotions that my body can feel, even (maybe especially) the "good" feelings, always scares the shit out of me.

As it happened, I did get drunk and eat chocolate (the little black dress, one of many, would come a bit later). And I managed to buy a bike.

The bike wasn't just any old Schwinn. It was a French-made Peugeot women's touring bike. It was painted metallic burgundy with "Peugeot" in decal on the down-tube in yellow-and-orange italic capitals, and on the stem was the Peugeot logo with the growling lion. It was *French*, which meant a lot to a girl who had grown up in American Strip-Mall Land where Schwinn and Sears were the best brands you could get.

I convinced myself I was investing in this French bike to save money on bus fare, because I was so poor I was seriously counting every last frigging dollar. But if I were just commuting back and forth to campus, I could have spent ten bucks on a Huffy junker. Instead, I scoured the want ads (remember those?) and found, waiting for me in the wilds of the western Pennsylvania suburbs, this barely used European bike—originally bought, to add to its exoticism, in the Hudson Valley, north of what some of my friends called The City. It was selling for $125, about $250 in today's dollars, a fortune for me then.

What's more, I'd never even ridden a real bike. The last bike I'd owned was the one I'd ridden in the sixth-grade bike-hike fundraiser. My sister had owned a ten-speed in high school, but in my two dozen years, I'd never managed a bike with more than one gear. This French bike had eighteen speeds with stem-mounted lever-shifters that looked like little twin chrome tongues sticking out at me and that I had no idea how to use. Touring bikes are engineered to produce minimal resistance and maximum forward momentum to conserve energy on long rural rides. This bike had center-pull caliper brakes. It had a high leather seat. It had leather-wrapped toe clips to keep my feet secure on long rides (presumably through flat, sunflower-studded French countryside).

I loved it as soon as I saw it without understanding why, and I sprang for it on the spot. The first time I managed, gasping and sweating, to pedal it up one of Pittsburgh's many hills, I experienced one of the powers greater than myself that I have respected ever since: gravitation. The earth's gravity dictates that what goes up has to come down, and this aluminum-alloy bike could fly. As soon as I shelled out for a speedometer, I found out that if I worked with gravity I could make the bike careen thirty-five miles an hour down one of the longer grades in my part of the city—ten miles an hour above the speed limit on that stretch, a pace that when I manage it today still makes the hair stand up on the nape of my neck and my voice scream with the relief of physical release.

I rode that bike every day during the summer of 1989. I remember telling a friend it was "my psychic salvation."

Since I couldn't booze and bike at the same time, I chose to drink less. And the more I rode, the less I seemed to want cookies. I wasn't watching my weight, yet by the time September rolled around, I had lost every ounce I'd put on in the spring and I was fitting into my clothes comfortably.

But what I loved most were the feelings that cycling gave my body. That summer I was working two jobs and writing on the side. I'd spend hours serving heavy dishes or sitting immobile in front of the computer, and afterward I felt iron fingers digging into my shoulders and lower back. Yet when I climbed onto the bike, all the worries—about money, success, love (what the hell else do we worry about?)—would roll off my shoulders. I gained strength and endurance. Soon I was timing myself on my eight-mile route, yelling in triumph when I'd break my own record. But the encouragement of the numbers aside, what satisfied me most was an experience that can't be measured: the opening of my senses. I came to know the neighborhoods and the passing of time on a daily basis by the smells of the outside world: honeysuckle at midnight in May, lilac at sunset in June, black locust on a July early morning. And through the scents of each season: cut grass in summer, rotting leaves in autumn, the smell of first snow. Soon my body began to crave not alcohol or sugar (which are pretty much the same thing), but the touch of the earth's beauty on my skin, inside my lungs, through my eyes.

I learned that I meet the world through my physical body. That's what I experienced back then, without entirely understanding what I was experiencing.

I don't think it was a coincidence that so many other productive things happened in my life during that time. That summer I wrote my first magazine piece, which was published that fall. I drafted the first section of my master's manuscript and gave a public reading to a packed house. I made new friends and moved into a bigger apartment. I had finally, for the first time in my life, really come home.

So what happened?

Easy. I stopped riding.

At the 2014 Clinton Foundation Health Matters conference in La Quinta, California, during a panel discussion on prescription drug addiction, National Institute on Drug Abuse (NIDA) director Nora Volkow offered an evolutionary explanation of why we members of *Homo sapiens* like drugs so much. "They can subvert—they hijack—a system that has taken millions and millions of years of evolution for nature to design, in order to make humans do behaviors that are crucial for their survival as individuals and as a species," she said. "And [drug use] does that by stimulating reward centers in the brain. That's why we eat, that's why we procreate, that's why we have social interactions. That's why we actually even move—it's highly rewarding."

So that's why I fell in love with my French bike that summer, because of the rewards—not just swift movement but also increased strength, improved physical appearance, and the motivation of competition, even if only with myself.

Researchers have long known that aerobic exercise is efficient at lifting one's mood, but it was only in the late-2000s that science finally admitted that this lift—the "runner's high"—was a result of exercise flooding the body with certain chemicals. Today it's often said that exercise stimulates the "reward centers," a term that's usually shorthand for the dopamine system, which is activated by stimulants, and the opioid system, which is activated by painkillers. Scientific research also indicates that the body's natural endocannabinoid system—the body's own cannabis or marijuana receptors—is responsible for the experience of relaxation, mood elevation, and suppressed pain sensitivity.

In the long-term, moving the body beats drugs hands-down in treating depression and anxiety. A 2012 Duke University study, for example, compared the effectiveness of Zoloft against running to treat depression. At four months, Team Zoloft and Team Hotfoot were neck and neck in terms of treating the illness: the drug was no more effective than exercise, and even putting the two together didn't boost any benefits. The real surprise in the results of this study showed up at long-term evaluations. A year after initiating treatment, one-third of those taking the drug had relapsed back into active illness; however, more than 90 percent of the runners were still in remission.

They were still running. They knew that moving their bodies was keeping them from relapsing. And as NIDA director Nora Volkow mentioned, evolution has made these behaviors feel good to provide incentive for us to do them. Movement *is* medicine.

"Exercise is the most overlooked critical element in most recovery processes," says Shane Niemeyer, an Ironman triathlete based in Boulder, Colorado, who uses physical fitness to help people in recovery. About half of Niemeyer's clients are senior executives in business who are recovering from addiction. "They just intuitively see the value of exercise," Niemeyer says. "I mean, it's pretty much a factual statement: your mental state and your emotional state parallel your physical state." So, he says, if you're "overweight and inert," you can expect that your feelings and your mind will follow your body.

The experience Niemeyer speaks from is unique, and nearly tragic. In 2003, at twenty-seven, he was arrested in Idaho for drug possession and burglary. In jail, he tried to hang himself and failed. He woke up wrapped in a straitjacket in a jail infirmary, a position that gave him a lot of time to think. While there, he came across some magazine stories about triathletes. He turned the pages with his toes (seriously!), and he decided that since killing himself hadn't worked out, he'd, well, he'd become a triathlete. And he did, in a process documented in his 2014 book *The Hurt Artist: My Journey from Suicidal Junkie to Ironman*. Since 2010, Shane has qualified for and competed each October in the Ironman World Championships in Kona, Hawaii.

"If you're inert, if you're inactive, it necessarily follows that you can't be truly happy or healthy," he says. "I mean, you just *can't*, right? Because who we are as sentient beings and who we are cognitively—we are tied to our bodies. That's what our organism is designed for. It's designed for movement."

And lack of movement is, as Harvard sociology professor Daniel Lieberman notes in this chapter's opening epigraph, abnormal and pathological. My mistake back in late 1989 had been to stop cycling. What can I say? Winter hit. These were the days before UnderArmour and Smartwool outerwear, before spats and gaiters and balaclava bike helmets, before Gold's Gym or 24 Hour Fitness. I couldn't have afforded any of those anyway.

It never occurred to me that I could use my free student pass to the university's gym. The idea of lifting weights had drifted through my mind, but the university gym was where the football and basket-ball teams trained, and the only people I had ever known who had lifted weights were dudes. *Therefore,* I concluded in my classic self-limiting way, *lifting must be for dudes.* Running is cheap, but I didn't believe I could run. I didn't even believe I could do sit-ups or pull-ups. The vestige of that chubby, sweaty, gasping little girl unable to finish her bike laps was still too powerful inside me, and I didn't see any other fitness options.

The same was true when I got sober in 2008. By then, I had in fact cycled through the sunflower-studded fields of France. I had hiked through the Rocky Mountains, the Appalachians, the European Alps, the Yorkshire Dales. I had practiced yoga. I had created a garden by double-digging a huge perennial border. In double-digging, you shovel the black topsoil off the clay subsoil, remove six inches of clay, shovel the topsoil back into the bed, then fertilize the heavy clay, and shovel all that back on top. Double-digging is a ton of work, and I'd accomplished all that without a rototiller.

But in detox, it had been years since I'd moved my body in those ways. I was insomniac and deathly tired, and my brain was muddled. I had trouble thinking through the simplest questions. I hadn't the first clue about how to recover my body.

It would have helped if I'd had some kind of community. There are loads of people in Twelve Step programs, for example, who exercise. Fitness is becoming increasingly popular among sober people.

"In the beginning, it's you introducing me to the bike that's the transformation. You have this confidence in me that I don't have yet," says Scott Strode, thirty-six, an athlete with sixteen years sober. Strode is founder of Phoenix Multisport, a Boulder, Colorado–based organization that sponsors climbing, hiking, running, swimming, biking, and other outdoor activities for people in recovery and people who choose to live sober. "The pushing through the hard times, the discipline of training, getting up on cold, wet mornings—we start to build this sort of strength that we carry into other aspects of our lives."

Strode says an enormous part of his early recovery was joining a local boxing gym in Boston, where he was living when he got sober. "Many of these guys were sober themselves because they were training for upcoming fights or they were struggling with addiction in their own lives," he says. "They essentially became my support system." Ice-climbing and mountaineering in the New England ranges gave him a sense that he could, he says, "overcome adversity if I put my mind to it. This belief in myself translated to my recovery as well." He started competing in triathlons, and with eight years sober he began to think about how he could give away what he had. Phoenix Multisport has expanded from Boulder to Colorado Springs and Denver, where the facility is located in "the epicenter of the homeless population," Strode says. "Here, Phoenix Multisport happens in the gym—people hitting heavy bags, doing yoga and CrossFit"—workouts made up of a variety of disciplines, including strength training, jump training, interval training, and gymnastics. Strode says the members working out in the gym derive the same benefits as those encountering the outdoors: "You can still build the same group of friends around a dry-erase board for CrossFit as you can climbing up a hill."

Soon Strode will open a location in Orange County, California. The organization has added 2,000 people per year in the last couple of years, and it's not just a hard-ass dudes' club: women make up about 40 percent of its membership. In 2012, CNN chose Strode as one of its heroes—"everyday people changing the world."

Having spent years working out with at-risk youth in New England, Strode learned that, for example, "Outward Bound has been using the outdoors to transform people for a long time. But I'd never seen it used specifically for recovering addicts. It was about me for a while; then it became about how I show up in the world for everyone else. Phoenix forges a lot of pretty deep friendships. Just knowing that we come from the same place—that brings a calm and opens up a space to build friendship."

Yeah, Strode is definitely onto something. And that's what I needed—community.

But when I started my recovery, not yet off Suboxone, I was told that my sponsor was not my higher power, that meetings would not save me, and that I'd only get really clean and sober through "prayer." So I spent a lot of time by myself, thinking and writing. The only community of sober people I had was online. They were dedicated and loving, and I remain indebted to them. Several I would trust with my house, car, and kid. But I could not look into their eyes, hold their hands, or stand shoulder to shoulder with them day after day, week after week. In my experience, it's that physical contact that busts down self-hatred.

Today it's possible to get at-home support for exercise regimens with online communities such as MyFitnessPal, Blogilates, thousands of exercise videos on YouTube, and the various forums set up by the makers of fitness trackers and home exercise programs. But in 2008, when I quit drugs, smartphones were Steve Jobs's brand-new baby and apps were only twinkles in developers' eyes. It wasn't until after I relapsed at the beginning of 2010 that I realized Jen would have to Get Her Ass Body Moving. Turns out, for me, and for a lot of others in recovery, it's hard to recover one's feelings and spirit without also recovering the body. And it's easier to do that alongside other bodies.

So that was my second mistake: I had tried to recover by myself.

"I think it helps if newcomers find a community that's going to exercise with them. I think throwing them into the gym with no support and nobody else who knows what they're doing—their chances aren't very good that they're going to continue," says Heather Henretig, house manager and chef at Chapters Capistrano, a drug and alcohol detox and rehab in southern California. Heather got sober at Safe Harbor Treatment Center for Women in Costa Mesa in 2010, after her addiction had progressed to the point that she had found herself living for two years in a crack house in her hometown outside Seattle, Washington. She used any drug she could get her hands on, she says, and her favorite was heroin.

Because I "only" ever used prescription painkillers, many of which are stronger than street drugs, I asked Heather why heroin still carries such a mystique. Although as of this writing, really pure heroin has become readily available and is sending people to emergency rooms, heroin is now cheaper, sometimes weaker, and easier to get than pills. What is still so badass about heroin?

"When people in AA [Alcoholics Anonymous] describe their first drink as that 'Ahhh' moment when everything is right with the world—for me that was opiates. And heroin is just the quickest, best way to get that feeling immediately," she says. "It's absolutely *immediate.*"

So the power is in the delivery. My drugs were never immediate. I didn't snort or inject my pills, so the fastest I could make them take effect was twenty minutes. And for that to happen, I had to starve myself and chew them so they'd go down as powder on an empty stomach. Later, when I was taking fentanyl, drugs hardly ever did anything for me except numb me out and stave off withdrawal—otherwise known as dopesickness. (I never thought of it as being "dopesick." In typical bourgeois terms, I thought of it as "Needing To Take Something" that would "Make Me Functional.")

Listening to Heather, I'm glad I never shot up, because if I had, I know it would be roughly four hundred thousand times harder than it is now for me to stay clean. I know, theoretically, that I could get some heroin about six blocks north of my house. Several times, in hopes of staving off dopesickness, I took my car cruising to see if I could figure out how to buy heroin. I mean, picture this: a white soccer mom driving a Subaru, with the sweat of desperation dripping down her sides and "Easy Target" tattooed across her forehead. How was someone like me gonna figure out how to score? I had seen the movie *Trainspotting* (I had not just "seen"

Trainspotting; I had watched it obsessively enough to memorize a good deal of the dialogue). My cousin had died of endocarditis, an inflammation of the heart, from years of injection drug use. I knew what heroin addiction looked like. So even while I was crawling along in my car through the streets in hopes of fixing my wretched cravings, I had images in the back of my mind of the risks of starting up with badass "H." I suppose I could say that a kind of primitive need to protect the safety of my body and to stay alive for my kid saved me from being raped, cut to ribbons, or for that matter actually shooting smack.

Heather did not escape such a fate. She lived inside the crack house with her dealer, a fat slob who wore beaters and boxer shorts, smacked Heather around, and screened porn videos around the clock. To get her next fix, Heather made her body do things that still haunt her. Finally, with a great deal of trepidation and with preparation from a professional recovery coach, Heather's mother—who never gave up on her daughter—rescued her and took her to spend two weeks in a medically managed detox facility in California. Then Heather went to live at Safe Harbor, where she later became a counselor.

"I remember the first day of treatment," Heather says. "We went on this little hike. And two of the girls decided to run. I was like, 'Okay, I'll try running.'" Heather had played varsity soccer and tennis for four years in high school, so she had run her share of laps. The idea of running was familiar in her mental memories, but her body, wasted from drug use, could no longer carry out her will. "I just about died. I was so out of shape; it had been so long since I had run."

Now, at thirty-two, almost four years off drugs and fed by excellent food that she cooks for herself and for the residents at the treatment center where she works, Heather says her body is more fit than it was fifteen years ago when she was training for competitive sports. She works out every day, starting with a two- to three-mile run, usually interspersing sprinting, jogging, and running uphill on a treadmill. Then she jumps rope. "I bring my jump rope everywhere I go," she says. Finally she lifts weights. She takes the rehab's residents to the gym twice a week and works out with them.

Because she had played sports, she says, the cognitive- and muscle-memory enabled her to understand what to do to recover her body. With people who have just kicked or gotten sober, she says, "Having someone show them what to do helps them. Because one thing that prevents people from working out is that they don't know what to do and they feel overwhelmed. And we addicts get overwhelmed easily."

She has a personal membership at a different gym at which many of the members, she says, just happen to be in long-term recovery. Granted, she lives in Orange County, home of the U.S. Open of Surfing and, like Boulder and other western locales, a mecca for outdoor sports enthusiasts and fitness fans. That is the reason Strode has chosen Orange County for his next Phoenix Multisport location.

"People in [recovery] like to work out, and I can't imagine Orange County is the only place where it's like that," Heather says, and she's right. "But it's kind of like a camaraderie—I have all my buddies there. Most of them are in the program. It's kind of like a social gathering place. It's a community, and I like that aspect."

But what if you can't afford a gym membership? Gyms are convenient because they have equipment in one space, Heather says, but "you don't have to go to the gym. You don't need to spend any money." She urges folks to find others in their area who also want to exercise. There's a guy who works out in the park next to her house; a couple times a week she'll join him. "All we have are resistance bands," she says—the cheap, portable, colored elastic bands with handles on both ends that can be used instead of expensive, heavy weights. "And I get a better workout there, sometimes, than I do with the machines."

After I relapsed at the beginning of 2010, I decided I'd have to do something different if I were going to stay sober. By that time it had been well over a year since I'd detoxed, and the post-acute withdrawal symptoms—restless legs, insomnia, my body's inability to regulate its own temperature, and deadening fatigue—had largely settled down. As I took stock, however, I had to admit to myself that, although I was no longer wide awake at night, I wasn't truly sleeping well and, even though I didn't feel as though my body were a sack of sand I was dragging around, I didn't feel much real energy. I realized that, although I'd begun riding a stationary bike during my active detox, I had long since quit that too. I'd rather exercise outdoors, and I hate using machines.

Then that spring my friend Julie asked me to play tennis with her.

I hadn't picked up a tennis racquet in more than twenty years, since I'd stopped seeing my college boyfriend Dave. He had played varsity tennis, and with an enormous supply of patience, he had taught me to play when we met in freshman year. He had helped me acquire the only racquet I'd ever owned until then—an oversized Head model in aluminum. *They don't even make them like that anymore,* I thought. I wondered whether the racquet was still floating around in the basement. Dave had believed I was actually capable of learning to play, and he had been right: I'd taken to it like a greyhound to the fields. By the end of the first year of his instruction, I could sometimes ace him with my serve. He took the little girl who had been chosen last for every team and found inside her the seed of a woman who enjoyed sports.

But a funny thing happened in my mind while I was learning to play tennis. Despite all the evidence to the contrary—Dave's surprised grins when I'd ace him, the college tennis coach asking me to try out for the women's team, and last and always least, my own enjoyment—I'd never "believed" I could play any sport. So that's what I kept telling myself. So I didn't try out for the team. I didn't play with anyone but Dave and his family. And when I lost contact with them, I stopped playing.

When Julie asked me to join her on the courts, I dug out my metal racquet from a cobweb-covered corner of the cellar and cleaned it off. Julie was a real beginner and, I thought, so was I. But once on court, I realized the benefit, the priceless gift, of excellent early instruction. Good form and habits are hard to learn for any sport, and I'd already learned them years before. It was spooky. I could feel the old movements and instincts Dave had ingrained in me still living inside my body. I kept looking around for him. It was almost as though he were there on the other side of the net, shouting the same advice he used to call to me years before. Good advice that I needed to hear then and I still need to hear now, on and off the court:

Loosen your grip.

Watch the ball.

Follow through.
Don't be afraid.
Relax.

I had "believed" I couldn't play tennis—but in spite of my "belief," in spite of my negative attitudes about myself and my capabilities, my body had so thoroughly learned how to play that its muscle movements came back to me after a hiatus of more than twenty years.

Or rather, I came back to my body after such a long absence.

In almost the same way, I had "believed" I could never get sober, and yet my body had gotten sober. When I freed my body of addictive chemicals, I could come back into it and recover my feelings, attitudes, values.

I hear people in recovery quite often asking how to "believe" in God/Higher Power/Whatever when you can't see it, when that power doesn't talk back. I think about my approach. "Approach" is another tennis strategy—another way to gain advantage over the opponent. In recovery, my opponents are obsession, delusion, the critical conference in my head—the so-called Itty Bitty Shitty Committee. Today, my approach to "God" is this: I try not to pay much attention to what I "believe." Would it have mattered what I "believed" about my athletic abilities if I had just put one foot in front of the other and kept playing tennis? What matters is what I do and how much I practice. The ways in which I hit the shots, turn my body, lean into the ball. How dedicated I am to staying fit and keeping my body and mind moving.

And I remember that, whatever I do, no matter how much I practice or how dedicated I am to staying fit, I'm bound to hit the ball out of bounds or double fault. I will miss the mark. I'm human and I screw up. To think otherwise is to participate in the great delusion, that maddening ongoing saga of perfection my addiction likes to write in my mind.

Humans are, as Nora Volkow mentioned, evolved to move, and drugs hijack the natural reward system that makes movement so gratifying. Which means that—*awesome!*—if we exercise, we can feel just as high as we did while we were on drugs. Right?

But exercising in recovery is not about counter-hijacking the reward system. It's about re-establishing a foundation of fitness that helps us conduct our lives from a position of stability and strength. A position of physical and emotional alignment.

A few months after I returned to tennis, I started to notice this strange feeling in my body. It was as though it *needed* to move. It was sort of an itch that could only be scratched if I exercised enough to sweat and breathe heavily for at least forty-five minutes. (This is what Dave taught me. I can remember him saying, "Anything that makes you sweat is aerobic exercise." The fact that he had to teach me this tells you how sedentary my childhood had been and how little I understood the body's need to move.) This desire to move and play was an appetite. I noticed that after I came home from the court, my muscles would be pleasantly sore, and I was hungry for food like chicken, kale with lemon, arugula with red peppers, pine nuts, garlic—not M&Ms or even those chocolate-covered emulsified-protein-pellet bars that are really just candy. (Toward the end of my addiction, I used to subsist on those bars—they made me "believe" I was eating "health food.") After playing tennis, I also slept more soundly than I did when I hadn't been exercising.

I played tennis into the fall, but inevitably the temperatures dropped and I could no longer play or ride my bike. Thanksgiving rolled around, my body began to resist settling down into sleep, and I felt cold all the time. By Christmas I had basically dived headfirst into the candy aisle in the grocery store. Ah, hell—holidays call for letting your hair down, right? But I had begun to despair of really testing the limits of my body's strength. As 2010 wound down and, without exercise, my body started to wind up like a spring, I thought about joining a gym. But I didn't want to have to get dressed up to work out, and I didn't want to spend time commuting to and from a gym, or working out in front of huge windows, or comparing myself with people with 10 percent body fat who worked out in Lycra clothes with expensive logos that never cut into their hips and back. I wanted a system that would allow me to exercise at home and slot my workouts into the narrow spaces that appear irregularly in my very busy days.

So I emailed Darlene.

Here's a perfect example of how recovery has changed me and the way I interact with the world: I'm now able to reach out to virtual strangers and ask for their help. This is because my friends in my system of recovery have repeatedly kicked my ass, urging me to talk to strangers at every meeting I attend. "You see somebody you don't know, you shake their hand," it has been suggested to me, and I do it even though I'm naturally shy because I can see it works for them. Now it works for me—though, even as I write this, with four years sober, I still can hardly "believe" it. I've spent more than four decades trying to do everything on my own, and I can see it's going to take more than a few years of action to turn that around.

I knew Darlene in high school. Which is to say, I *knew of* her. I don't think I ever spoke a single word to her, although of course her voice, her brilliant blonde-framed face with dimples on either side of her perfect smile had seemed to me to be omnipresent in our school. She circulated high in the food chain: she was one of the student government officers, and she didn't just "date" the varsity quarterback—he was her *boyfriend.* That kind of girl. I was this kind of girl: National Honor Society and advanced placement, first-chair flute in the marching band—the un-glam crowd, pure freak material. Darlene was part of that fair, blue-eyed stratosphere of cheerleaders and prom-court babes who never mixed with the likes of geek-squad girls like me.

Or so I thought. Was that really the way it was? Who was making assumptions about whose history here? Who was labeling whom "worthy" and "unworthy"?

I "friended" Darlene cold on Facebook shortly after I relapsed, when I came across some of her posts and saw that they coincided with mine in politics and humor. And to my surprise, she accepted. (*Like omg, why would Darlene accept my FB friend request?* my suspicious post-adolescent mind babbled.) Then a couple months later, while I was playing tennis, she started P90X, a rigorous home-exercise regimen, and she sometimes posted updates.

When tennis stopped and winter hit that year, I knew I had to get serious about exercise. So I wrote to Darlene, who is now a business consultant, a mom, and still miraculously, stratospherically beautiful. This time she gave me her cell number. When we talked, she corrected me: "I was never a *cheerleader*, I was on the drill team," the group of girls who danced in front of the marching band during halftime shows. So that's where I remembered her from. I'd stood behind her, playing the music while she danced in her miniskirt and white go-go boots. She also said she'd never been an athlete, although having a quarterback boyfriend meant many of her friends had been athletes. So she herself had been leery about trying a strenuous exercise system. She swore it had changed not only the way her body looked and felt, but also the way her mind operated. She had more confidence. Which, I was like, *Does somebody like you really need More Confidence?* But what does that mean, "Somebody Like You"? Ultimately, what do I know about Darlene's life? What I know about me is that I'm excellent at judging books by their covers. Enacting the opposite of this shortcoming means practicing tolerance and humility and giving people the benefit of the frigging doubt.

"Listen, if I could do this, you can too," she said. *Maybe she was a cheerleader after all,* I thought. Actually, what she proved to be, over the ensuing months, was an effective and dedicated coach.

"If you want," she said that first day, "I'd be glad to give you moral support. I mean I'm happy to talk on the phone, trade emails—whatever it takes to help you do this."

All this openness and willingness, and we had never talked before.

Why does it still stagger me that when I ask for help I usually get it, and with such generosity? This remains one of the great "miracles" of my recovery. The origin of the word "miracle" doesn't mean that the magician snaps his fingers and the lame dude picks up his mat and walks home, or the geek morphs into a cheerleader. It means, simply, something amazing, wonder-full. *Awe-some.*

For offering such dedicated help regarding my fitness, I don't think anyone would have called Darlene "evangelical" or "religious." But when people in recovery offer this kind of help in healing from an illness, we're branded New-Age Unscientific Evangelical Crackpots. When I joined Darlene's little team that day, I realized that recovery communities are more like teams than religions. I choose a coach who tells me how many laps to run, how much progress she thinks I'm making, how to play the game the way she learned it. I pick teammates who work out alongside me and play along with me, sharing strategies and experiences. We win some and we lose some, and we remember that it's just a game, so we don't take ourselves too goddam seriously. Then we shower up, chase each other around and slap each other with wet towels in the locker room, and go out and do life.

I came up with two simple goals in my fitness program.

         Goal 1: test my strength.

         Goal 2: do an unassisted pull-up before I died.

That's seriously how long I figured it would take me. The mental image of the ten-year-old girl struggling to maintain the flexed-arm hang for even five seconds, the feeling of her sweaty palms slipping off the rusty steel monkey bars, the taste of dust after she hit the dirt—all that was so vivid that I figured I'd be at least seventy-five before I lifted my chin over the bar. And then I'd probably croak out of sheer shock. That is, if the workouts themselves didn't kill me.

With Darlene's help, I kept my commitment to exercise six days a week for twelve weeks. For as much as the regimen challenged me physically, it tested me at least as much mentally and emotionally. The first day I had to do "dive-bomber" push-ups, which must have been invented by some high-paid former Texas Jarhead dipping Skoal and guzzling Red Bull. "Let's make her do downward dawg," he must have growled to himself, "and make her keep her hands and feet superglued to the mat, and then make her pretend she has to squeeze under a barbwire fence with a coyote chasin' her! And let's make her do it forwards and backwards! Let's repeat the rounds and see how many she pulls off after tryin' wide-flies and military-style and diamond push-ups! *Haaaaahahaha*," I can hear him cackling as he knocks back the dregs of Red Bull, spits his chaw juice into a coffee can and pictures me crashing on my head. Which is exactly what happened. My arms would not hold me up, despite all the signals my brain was sending, and I fell on my face.

This is when I almost gave up the entire deal. Yeah, on the first day.

It reminded me so much of Almost Giving Up on my first days sober.

I almost said "Fuck It." While I was on my belly, having bit the mat, I could hear the ass-hat high school gym teacher calling me an Old Lady from the other side of the football field while she hobnobbed with the track stars who had already finished their four laps and were sauntering in for their showers. *"Fuck It."*

Famous last words. Also the words I said to myself before I stole Vicodin and chewed and dry-swallowed it in my relapse.

I decided to keep showing up, after receiving some encouragement from Coach Darlene, who, ironically, gave me the same kind of rhyming advice we get in recovery ("attitude of gratitude," etc.).

"Do your best," Darlene said, "and forget the rest."

Jesus wept.

"It's called a ninety-day program for a reason," she said.

Anyone for 90 meetings in 90 days?

But if I couldn't even try another dive-bomber push-up without breaking my nose, how was I ever going to have a chance of getting better at anything? If your best totally sucks, how can it ever improve?

It's called "recovery."

Here's what happens in fitness. What makes the muscles so sore is that they develop tiny little microtears. If you're cross training—working out different parts of the body on different days, which is what I was doing—then during the week when you give the muscles a break and exercise other parts of the body, those tiny little tears heal. The body's inherent ability to heal itself makes the muscles stronger. It is called "recovery" because the muscles literally recover.

The body recovers.

In the meantime, you're also raising the levels of endorphins and dopamine in the body. You're reregulating the body's metabolism—its capacity to burn energy efficiently. You're not just exercising biceps and triceps and deltoids or even chest, back, legs, and core. You're also exercising the internal organs: heart, lungs, circulatory system, central nervous system (including the brain), digestive system. You're even exercising the skin by making it sweat. Sweating, as many people now know, is a great way to rid the body of toxins—those substances that make us "in*toxic*ated."

You're also exercising the will, the psyche, the spirit. The "heart" (as in, "That quarterback has a lot of heart").

This happens even when you're forty-six, which I was, and you've been telling yourself for more than thirty years that you're not capable of real physical fitness because you're an "old lady."

At the end of the first week, I noticed I was standing taller. My body felt warmer. I woke in the mornings feeling as if I'd slept soundly—because I had. The second week in, I did eleven of those goddam Dive-Bomber Push-Ups.

"Dude," I hollered downstairs to my son as soon as I did them, "I just did *eleven* of those things that made me crash on my head last week."

My son hollered back, *"Yeah, my Main Mama!"*

When I wrote Darlene, she replied, "Yeah, baby!! I am SO STOKED FOR YOU" (read with a Spicoli accent).

Our Facebook interactions were becoming longer and more personal, and eventually I decided I wanted to be real with Darlene about why I was trying this exercise program. So I told her about my addiction and sent her some links to my blog. Then I held my breath for a few days until she wrote back: "I feel we are becoming friends beyond the Facebook sense, and that is important to me. Your addiction is, in my mind, not much different than if you told me you had an ongoing illness you are battling."

Which seems like a great analogy, because it's not even an analogy: that's what addiction is—an ongoing illness.

Then she blew me away by mentioning her brother has been an alcoholic and drug addict for most of his life. This turned my Perfect Prom-Court Babe image of her not upside down, but instead into a flesh-and-blood human being whose history was written in pain and cracks in her heart similar to my own.

"Shit, for real—isn't perception *crazy*?" she said.

I told her how much her words of encouragement had meant to me when I was about ready to give up.

"I'm amazed to know how a simple couple of words from me made a difference," she said. "That's hard to comprehend, but a tremendous lesson in practicing care and thoughtfulness in every interaction we have.

You never know where a person is in life and how you can have a positive or detrimental impact."

About six weeks into the ninety-day program came the day I pulled my chin over the bar without leaning a foot on the chair. It was like looking out from a porthole of the space shuttle and seeing Earth. An entirely new perspective on myself and my world opened up. I began to wonder, *What else do I believe I cannot do?*

I had begun exercising to sleep better and scratch that internal physical itch that told me to get my body moving. After exercising for a year or so, my motivation changed. I began to do it because it brought me back to my body, which brought me back to the truth—of my life, of myself.

The people I spoke with who either had been athletes in their youth or who were familiar with exercise agreed that in sobriety their motivations about working out changed from their original, more shallow intentions—otherwise they couldn't have carried on with it.

"Something I've noticed is that when we first get sober, we want to focus on the external right away," Heather, the treatment center house manager, said. "We want to get our hair done; we want to start looking better. And so I think deep down, part of starting to exercise again was maybe my ego. Vanity, totally."

But she also said that her experience in youth with soccer and tennis had largely been a result of her parents talking her into playing sports when she was a little girl. "It's what I did because it was expected of me by my parents," she said. "So I think my exercise regimen is different now because it's on my own terms. And because I certainly don't make the gym my higher power."

My friend Nicole, who ran Division I track at Syracuse University at the same time as her addiction was taking hold, said she has learned in recovery that her fitness practice is about "awareness on a very deep level." As she speaks about this, I notice, she's sort of digging at her sternum with her fingertips—the place, as some yoga instructors would say, where her "heart chakra" is located. Nicole is now sober nine years, a personal

fitness consultant, and a yoga practitioner with a growing list of corporate and individual clients. She runs a private downtown gym. She still
runs and lifts weights, but it was, in fact, yoga that taught her the deep
awareness she mentions.

And even her ideas about yoga had to change. Her first experience
with yoga had been as an elective at Syracuse, and "I hated it," she says.
"It was this old hippie woman, and when you're twenty-one, 'Lion's Breath'
is not the thing that's gonna turn you on. Plus, I was also into the adrenaline at that point, and yoga wasn't going to do that for me."

Later, during her sobriety, after she had gained some clean time, she
went to live with a friend in recovery, whose daughter came back from
college and took Nicole to a power-flow yoga studio where she learned
vinyasa yoga, a style that links postures into a continuous flowing movement. "I was in really good shape at the time. I was running and weight
training, but after that one yoga session, my body was sore for a week, and
that felt like I was obviously working some muscles out that I didn't know
about." So she went back.

"Yoga changed my life," she says.

A critical element of yoga practice is learning to pay attention to and
regulate one's breath. The word "yoga" is Sanskrit that means, literally,
"yoked" or "united," and this is often taken to mean the unity of mind and
body. Another interpretation of the word, however, is "to concentrate,"
and the Yoga Sutras, the ancient texts that describe the forms and philoso-
phy of the practice, say the purpose of yoga is to still the ripples of the
mind. Yoga practitioners do this, my yoga teacher Christina says, by concentrating the body on healing positions while concentrating the mind on
the breath.

And then doing it again, and again. Because, in a kind of fundamental way, exercise is just like taking a drink or a drug: to feel it solving our
problems, we can't just do it once. We have to do it regularly. Exercise conditions our bodies and minds together.

Which makes it understandable to hear the way Nicole talks about
exactly how long it took for her yoga practice to change her life. "About
two years into it," she says, "I started to notice that the breathing they
teach you as part of a vinyasa practice was happening automatically. It

was so automatic that I realized my body had learned something with-out my knowing it." Just as, while learning tennis in college, my body had learned about the discipline and pleasure of athleticism without my knowing it. "Then I started to think more about yoga outside of yoga class," Nicole continues, "and I realized that yoga is one of the only things I can do where I can be fully focused on one thing and my mind can be quiet. Not even running can do that for me." Running, Nicole says, some-times magnifies her feelings, and she ends up emotionally overwhelmed. But her yoga practice demanded she let go of thinking about anything other than her breath and her body. "Yoga was the opposite of running," she explains. "It was so challenging for me to *only* be in that place, and to *only* be in that moment. I had to concentrate so I didn't fall off my one-hand balance, and I loved that.

"Yoga started showing up in all areas of my life. Like, 'Okay, this is a difficult moment—just breathe and concentrate.'

"You could look at my life and say, 'You exercised before you got sober, and you exercise now—what's different?'" she adds. "The difference is really the awareness that I have within myself."

Nicole says the discipline of yoga practice helped her understand she has two voices that motivate her. On the one hand, she says, "One side is the young, scared child that doesn't trust anybody, doesn't believe that my needs will ever be met, and thinks the world sucks at large. That also turns into an adult voice—it's like a very driving voice—that says, *You must go, go. You must do, do, do.* It tells me no matter what I do, I'm never gonna be good enough.

"Then there's this other side that is a recent development for me," she says. "It's like a nurturing voice. It's like my authentic Self with a capital S. It's the part that says, *You know what, Nicole? You've been through a lot. Give yourself a break.*"

"Yoga kind of backdoored Nicole," says Jenn, a mutual friend of Nicole's and mine. "She went for the physical practice, and the other por-tions of the practice kind of schooled her."

My friend Jenn Ferris-Glick, also in her early thirties, had her first drink when she was seven. "My grandfather would make us what he called Shirley Temples, but they would be like peach schnapps and grenadine and Sprite." She rolls her eyes and makes a face. "He would also save the olives in his vodka martinis—when they would be soaking in that vodka—and he would have four of them in his glass, one for each of his granddaughters. I mean, I think it was just because we all liked olives. I don't think he realized that feeding us vodka-soaked olives was maybe not appropriate."

A high-strung high achiever, Jenn depended more and more on alcohol to calm herself down and even just to get some sleep. Then she'd load up on caffeine in the mornings, which only compounded her anxiety and threw her body into panic attacks with heart palpitations. Once, in high school, she experienced a caffeine-induced paralysis in which the left side of her body went numb. She was drinking caffeine under the assumption that it would give her energy, but the energy caffeine "gives" the body is borrowed from the adrenal glands, which caffeine stimulates to produce adrenaline and cortisol—stress hormones that put our body into crisis-response mode and actually disrupt sleep. Far from helping the body adapt to stress, caffeine can damage its ability to respond to stress productively by creating a virtually constant state of fight-or-flight response. (And like alcohol, caffeine also prevents the body from absorbing nutrients, causing the body to leach them from bones and tissues.) To come back down from all that caffeine, Jenn would drink. And so the cycle continued.

This level of anxiety had a payoff for Jenn. "I felt like I was creative," she says. "It helped me feel like I was artistic, if you will. I know so many artists who have gone through something similar—'I don't want to give up my alcohol. I don't want to give up that disease for fear it'll change me.'"

When Jenn entered graduate school at Bucknell University in Lewisburg, Pennsylvania, she upped the ante by taking Vivarin (these were the days before Red Bull and "energy" drinks stood at every convenience store's cash register) and drinking even more, along with smoking lots of pot. "Pot made me hate people," she says with an amused smile. She broke up with a boyfriend because, she decided, she didn't like him when she was high, and she couldn't give up her pot, so the dude had to go. Finally she decided she had to try something different to ease her angst, so she bought some yoga DVDs. Whereas Nicole tried yoga for its physical relief and found emotional relief later, Jenn found emotional relief first.

"When I moved back to Pittsburgh, I'd go to yoga, right? And I would rush to get there after being at work all day." She works in the neuro-science lab at Carnegie Mellon University. "I was working sixty- and seventy-hour weeks because I needed to escape the relationship I was in." And because, like Nicole and many, many addicts, she needed to feel validated externally—by a job, a man, something other than herself and her values.

What she discovered through sticking with the emotional relief of the yoga stretches was the physical discipline of bringing her body to the yoga mat on a regular basis. Just as Nicole discovered her body breathing automatically and creating emotional relief, Jenn discovered that bring-ing her body regularly to the mat—in whatever hopped-up, stressed-out condition it was in—resulted in an emotional commitment to herself and her well-being that she had never known before. Through committing to herself, she began to perceive connections with others where, it had seemed, none had existed before.

"Now that I'm sober, now that I have a Higher Power, I have this alignment with my Self with a capital S," she says. "What I mean by 'Self with a capital S' is the knowledge that I am connected to every single thing in this entire universe. I am made up of the same particles of mat-ter as everybody else. I have the same insecurities and the same joys. And that knowledge runs deep through everybody—we hide that, we disguise it, we create these illusions that that isn't who we are. Now that I have that knowledge, my yoga practice, my embodiment practice, is totally transformed." *Embodiment:* em-body-ment. These days, for Jenn, reliev-ing anxiety is no longer about simply stretching and reducing her physi-cal tension. It's about bringing her body to her yoga mat and perceiving this connection with other human beings and with who she is as a person and how she walks around in this world. Jenn's perceptions and actions become clearer the longer she stays sober and continues these practices.

Many people who get their bodies moving as part of their recovery find out that the physical discipline teaches them about self-love, that Self with a capital S. "To me, it's a self-worth thing," Scott Strode of Phoenix

Multisport says. "How do I view myself? What sort of love do I have for myself?" He talks about the transformative power of physical movement. "When we achieve these goals, there's this really joyous response in the body," he says. "We light up those switchboards that were deadened by our addiction. We start to be able to be inside an emotion."

I'm purposely not offering a specific exercise regimen for anyone here. I'm telling these stories to demonstrate a variety of approaches to exercise. If you're stuck and looking for a way to exercise, you might look around you in your recovery community and see who's practicing yoga, who wears running shoes, who comes to a meeting carrying a bike helmet, and ask those people for suggestions about how to get moving. I've given examples of high-level and elite athletics, but for some of us, simply walking from thirty minutes to an hour a day will be a great start.

After working my way through two full ninety-day rounds of P90X, plus a summer of tennis and cycling, I finally began, in 2012, to run. I was three-and-a-half years out of detox. My son, Jonathan, who was fourteen at the time, was told to run two miles a day for his new high school soccer team. When I took him to the shoe shop, I had my own feet fitted. I tried on three pairs. "They should fit like gloves," the woman said. "You shouldn't be able to feel them." I shelled out more than I'd ever paid for any athletic shoes, and all I could hear in my head was my mother's voice when I'd put down thirty bucks in 1983 for the "new" used tennis racquet Dave had helped me find: *What a waste of money. You're supposed to be spending money on useful things like books, not tennis racquets. You're supposed to be working, not playing.*

Those of us with a perfectionistic streak and a bitchy internal critic have a real hard time playing at anything. It's difficult to sidestep or confront that internal critic; it's easier just to numb it out—or to give in and try to satisfy it while numbing out our own feelings of despair at the impossibility of that task. For years I took drugs so I didn't have to listen to that bitch on wheels tell me what I should or shouldn't be doing. Or I took drugs so I could do what she commanded and numb out my wretchedness that I'd once again sold myself out.

One of the best pieces of advice I've ever received with respect to physical training came from Dan Cronin, a sixty-something addictions interventionist based in Pasadena, California, who has more than twenty years sober from, as he says, "all of the above." Cronin races Ironman triathlons to raise money for the Veterans Health Initiative, which provides treatment for addicted vets. He has worked in substance abuse counseling for National Hockey League and Major League Soccer teams for more than a decade. ("Even when I was getting loaded, I've done fitness," he said, echoing the experience of a number of people I know in sobriety. Here are just two examples: Jenn started practicing yoga while she was drinking, and my good friend Benedick, a professor and Emmy Award–nominated director, began swimming in a men's masters club years before finally giving up booze and then weed.)

Cronin's helpful advice: "I give people a simple method of how to train. We're talking about people with obsessive qualities, right? They haven't run in ten years—and they're gonna go out and run a marathon tomorrow. I like Jeff Galloway's run-walk-run technique. I tell them, 'I want you to go out tomorrow and run whatever is comfortable for you, whether one or two or three minutes. I don't care how fast or slow. Then you walk for a minute. And you do that ten times. When you can do that comfortably, then up the number by another minute.'"

Rinse and repeat.

"That's all it takes to start building endurance," Cronin assures me.

In this way, I started running. I was playing tennis, for the first time, in a United States Tennis Association–ranked competitive league—unbelievable! I was cycling ten or fifteen miles at a time. It was when I found myself logging one hundred sixty full push-ups—on my toes—plus fifty more on my knees each time I did my push-up workout, that I began to ask myself why the hell I was doing all this exercise. I loved telling people, "I do *a hundred and sixty push-ups* each workout," and then watching their faces. They'd look me up and down in a way people had never looked at me before, with admiration and a tinge of envy. But what was the next goal—two hundred push-ups? What would it be after that? What was the Next Level in the game?

How many push-ups would be enough?

"I used to train at Gold's Gym," Cronin told me, "and it was horrendous to watch the women with eating disorders, and they're running with their hands over their heads so they can burn more calories." Meanwhile, he said, he'd attended an eating disorder conference at which the addictions specialists "were worse than the people we're trying to treat. They were obese, smoking cigarettes—it's like, what business are we in?"

For Shane Niemeyer, the convicted felon turned triathlete, "enough" exercise is a level that supports the body and makes it healthy. And he determines his body's "health"—wholeness—through maintaining an ongoing conversation with his body.

"I'm really in touch with my body now more than most people," Shane says. "But it's sometimes not a healthy level of exercise. I can be very fit, but at those times it's a question of how healthy I am. I can sometimes constantly ask myself, 'How symmetrical am I? Are my feet maintaining an even force to the ground? Are my hips cocked?' I'm very in touch with 'How tired am I? How does my tissue feel?'"

He asks his body how heavily it's meeting the ground, how well its bones are aligned, *how its tissues feel.* And then he listens to what his body has to say. But maybe, especially for addicts, even that level of attentive conversation with our bodies could turn into self-centered obsession. "Every elite athlete I know," Shane says, "they're all that way, because success necessitates that level of attention. The focus is very unilateral, and we become self-involved, always thinking about training and how we're feeling." And Shane works mostly with high-level executive addicts and alcoholics, who, like elite athletes, maintain that unilateral focus on success. Hell, how many of us haven't at one time or another believed that fame and/or fortune would not be the same kind of solution that drugs used to be? One sign that we're headed into obsession is discovering that such focus crowds out the activities that keep us healthy, especially harmonious and supportive relationships.

"In this country we have a sick view of what success is," Shane says. "With senior-level executives, it's so one-dimensional. They're always on their goddam iPhones. When they're home, they're never really at home."

I participate in those fantasies as much as anyone else does. I write myself into stories as the main character who overcomes some kind of enormous obstacle, wins praise from not just my dead parents (who, in the story, usually come back from the dead to tell me how awesome I am—as though that's the really important thing, talk about "miracle" total bullshit), and all my friends, but also from strangers in the grocery store, and especially from you. The Heroine who finally proves, without a doubt, that she is worth the three square feet of space her body occupies while it's standing up on this planet. Sometimes it takes crashing and burning to wake me up out of that self-involvement.

After a couple months of running two miles at a time, one fine spring afternoon I went for my "usual" run (by this time I liked to call it "my usual run," as in "I *usually* run two miles"), and I felt so awesome in the late-afternoon spring breeze that I decided I'd go another mile—or two. Or maybe five! I would prove that I was Really An Athlete the way the regulars up at the tennis courts had been telling me I was. I would brag to Ordinary People that I was now running *four miles a day,* and all this evidence (and bragging) would make me a total moron no, it would make me feel über-awesome about myself! I would prove to myself and to all these Other People that I was finally worthy of just being alive. After all, four miles is like a cross-country race, right?

I'd start racing.

I'd race in the 10K Komen Race for the Cure on Mother's Day, and by the end of the summer I'd be running half-marathons.

Never mind that I'd never run a race in my entire life.

Maybe only because you didn't want to race, my mind whispered.

With my eyes blinded not by the sun or the sweat fogging my glasses but by the future-tripping yarn I was spinning in my mind of Finally Being Worth Something, I passed my usual turnoff to my home and kept running on the sidewalk down a main drag in my city. And because I was not exactly paying attention to reality (to the truth, in other words), I wasn't looking at the pavement and the toe of one of my almost-new pink-and-white Asics Gel Sport running shoes caught on an uneven piece of concrete. I crashed onto my left knee, scraping my elbow. I waited a moment to feel the stabbing pain of a broken bone. Then when that failed to materialize, I sat up to inspect the damage. I have pretty bony knees; I had scraped the skin almost off my kneecap, and blood was coursing down my leg in jagged red rivulets. Gravel and dust were embedded in the thin flesh. I sat there panting on the sidewalk and could almost feel the little glands on top of my kidneys squeezing adrenaline into my body as I started to shake. I looked up and saw a guy walking toward me, so I uncertainly hauled my body upright, ready to tell him I was okay but if his car were anywhere near. . . .

"Hey hon," he said peremptorily, "can you tell me where the closest bus stop is?"

"Um," I said, limping a few steps, the blood running even more heavily down my leg. Didn't he see *the fucking blood,* for chrissake?—a resentment in the making.

"Yeah, it's around that corner," I said, pointing.

"Thanks!" he said cheerfully, his eyes scanning the street signs, and he wandered off.

Had I still been using, I would have been even more deeply entrenched in my own Fake World, and I would have seen none of the humor and irony of this exchange. I also would have more seriously expected someone else to take care of me instead of being ready to do that work for myself. Limping toward home, I noticed that what the scientists say about exercise and neurotransmitters was true. Despite the fact that I was bleeding like hell in two or three places and had left a good bit of skin on the sidewalk, I felt no pain at all until twenty minutes after the crash, when my body's natural drugs wore off. By that time I was in my kitchen, cleaning up.

Sometimes it takes longer to heal—from injury, from addiction—than we expect. My skin produced a raised, discolored scar on my kneecap, and it took a year for my body to heal it. I was so impatient to see the evidence of my "accident" recede and fade that I thought maybe I'd have to hire a plastic surgeon to fix it. Instead I waited. Turned out my body was quite capable of the mend. As long as I supported it, and didn't pick the scab.

You can still see evidence of my injury, though. The scar is like a finely crocheted silver net across my left knee. It shows when I wear shorts or skirts or when I take my clothes off, but I don't mind: It proves that I tried something. That I was out there, moving. Living. Instead of sitting at home, in one room, numbing my body. Abandoning myself.

Some Guidelines

Here are some guidelines to follow as you begin, or continue, to move the permanent home that is your body:

- Start where you are. Don't try to move too far, too much, too fast.
- Consult with a doctor, especially if you have health conditions that complicate your exercise plans.
- Good exercise doesn't require a gym membership or expensive equipment and clothing. There are plenty of free resources and low-cost equipment (resistance bands, yoga mats, etc.) that can help you get a routine started.
- Look to your recovery community for ideas, help, and support.
- Inquire into your own motivations for exercising: Is it to foster health and self-respect? Is it to impress others?
- Listen to your body's needs for movement.

Nourishing the Body
Appetite and Food

• •

People with addictive bodies love to "take something," be It pills,
white powder, or special mixtures from a can. "Taking something"
becomes the solution rather than creating a lifestyle with a healthy
relationship to food. Eating food as your solution to sugar sensitivity
or addiction demands that you think about what food you will eat.

–Kathleen des Maisons, author of *Potatoes Not Prozac*
and founder of Radiant Recovery

I used to wonder at what moment in my life I became an addict. What
was the dividing line? Taking OxyContin? But before that I'd taken morphine, which has a longer history with addiction. Before morphine, I'd
taken Vicodin, which is weaker, but which I'd chewed, so I had "abused"
it. Before those I'd taken codeine, Stadol, and barbiturates. If you want
to go back to the beginning, I had my first drink at seventeen—but even
though I got wasted, one night with a cheap gin and tonic didn't make me
an instant alcoholic.

It's equally impossible to tell exactly when someone contracts cancer.
The disease doesn't start at diagnosis—the treatment does. With many
types of cancer, by the time they are found, they've been growing inside

the body for years. The fact is, we're all living our days with cancer cells floating around in our blood—and the better we take care of our immune systems (ironically, with exercise, nutrition, sleep, pleasure, and mindfulness), the better we boost our bodies' ability to kill those stray cells.

But when I try to determine when the "stray cells" of addiction started to settle into healthy tissue and grow out of control, I think of one particular situation, and it had nothing to do with drugs as we think of them.

After school one afternoon back in the mid-1970s—I was ten or eleven—my mother made a batch of cupcakes. She took out a hand mixer, a wooden spoon, eggs, Wesson oil, and the plastic bowl into which she dumped the boxed Pillsbury or Duncan Hines cake mix. This was 1970s suburban American life: my mother hardly ever baked anything "from scratch," that is, from unpackaged ingredients.

She might have been baking these cupcakes for my sister's birthday. My little sister would have been in first grade, and Mom was always nice about making "goodies" for us to take to school. We weren't allowed to take in sticks of bubble gum or candy the way other kids did. Except for Easter (when she chose all the candy herself) and Halloween (when she checked every last Reese's Cup for razor blades), candy was *verboten* in our household. Dad had ruined his teeth on penny candy as a kid. But "goodies" were stashed in every nook and cranny: Twinkies, Ho Hos, Oreos, Chips Ahoy; those disgusting Little Debbie cupcakes that, if they weren't eaten fast enough, used to grow white fur inside their plastic wrapping. Mom baked only on special occasions, but she bought out the store when it came to "goodies."

So these homemade cupcakes must have been for a special occasion, and I would have been standing next to her at the counter in the tiny nook of a kitchen we had in our three-bedroom split-level house way out on the edge of the county. One of us kids always got to lick either the beaters, bowl, or wooden spoon, and I was waiting to see which I'd get. Whichever one it was, it apparently only whetted my appetite. On this day, I remember, the cake batter and icing were both chocolate. It was my favorite, always: the more chocolate, or the darker the chocolate, the more I liked whatever it was she was making, and the harder it was for me to stop eating it. Even raw.

Eventually my mother arranged the baked cupcakes on her 1950s scalloped glass cake plate and iced them with Pillsbury or Duncan Hines chocolate icing, mixing it up with the wooden spoon and spreading it with the black-handled square-tipped icing spatula. I got to lick either spoon, spatula, or bowl. After she finished, the cupcakes sat uncovered on the corner of the counter in front of the toaster, in a place where, every time I walked by, I had to look at their shiny deep brown swirls of icing. The temptation became overwhelming. I decided I would use my fingertip to swipe just a little bit of icing off the edge of one cupcake. Which "worked" until I passed the cupcakes again, and I decided to take another swipe off the edge of another cupcake.

Pretty soon I was standing in front of the plate, swiping all the icing off all the cupcakes.

The interesting thing here is the rationalization, the disconnect that took place in my mind as I carried out this half-baked, little-girl compulsion. I knew I'd get into trouble if anyone found out I was doing this. Still, I thought if I could just prevent anyone from catching me in the act of doing it, I could pull it off, and somehow no one would ever know.

I was engaging in the same theft and twisted logic thirty years later when I changed dates on prescriptions to buy refills of my drugs before they were due. *If only the pharmacist doesn't catch me in the act*, was my weird illogic, *I'll be home free. I'll have gotten one over on them again.* And every time I went home with drugs in my bag, the illogic was reinforced by the sheer adrenaline rush of *getting one over.* In fact, I became so fond of *getting one over* on someone—pharmacists, doctors, *the system*—that I'd go steal cheap shit just to feel the chemical rush of adrenaline through my blood: the pounding heart, the sweat, the lightheadedness. It was the closest I was letting myself get to passion in those days, and it cost me.

One day, after walking blithely out of a British drugstore with a bullshit piece of makeup worth ten quid in my pocket, the Leeds city cops picked me up, threw me in the back of a cruiser, drove me to the station, let me shed my crocodile tears in a cell, and booked me, scaring the shit out of me—I had tickets for a train to London that afternoon and a plane to the States the next day. After several hours, they released me with just a caution, and the offense has since been expunged from the books, but it remains engraved on my memory as one of a number of insane stunts I pulled as a direct result of my active addiction. The only other time I got picked up for shoplifting, I was in a U.S. strip mall and had stolen a crappy twelve-dollar set of earbuds I didn't need or even want. The security woman pulled me into a messy, windowless back room, shut the door, looked me up and down, noted my Coach bag and middle-class clothes, regarded the stolen property in her hand, and said slowly, "You need to seek help." I was appalled that this woman's paycheck was funded solely to protect the store from criminals and from sick people like me whose illnesses made them into criminals. Her declaration struck my ear as a Delphic voice that echoed in my mind until the next summer, when I finally hired a doctor to detox me.

Of course, with addiction, it never works out that you get one over on someone without consequences. It might seem at the time as if it *could,* but it never actually does. "Who the hell licked all these cupcakes bald?" my mother bellowed when she came down to make dinner. ("Bald" was one of her favorite words to describe something that was supposed to be covered with something else, but wasn't.) I confessed. Who else could it have been? My brother pulled some nutty stuff, but chocolate wasn't his thing, and my sister was just a sweet little girl who couldn't even reach that high. And my mother yelled, "What in god's name were you thinking?"

If she'd been alive to ask me what in god's name I was thinking when I changed dates on scripts, the answer would have been the same: "Well, Mum, I wasn't thinking; I was just doing what my addiction was telling me to do."

Like a lot of people with addiction I have known (including, it turns out, my father), my first chemical of abuse was sugar, my first addictive behavior was eating, and I have never managed to quit eating foods with added sugar for more than a couple of months.

Why (in god's name) do I eat sugar?

I eat it habitually, just because I Do.

I eat it because I've always eaten it.

I eat it to comfort myself when I'm upset, bored, happy, or sad. When I'm hungry, angry, lonely, or tired.

I eat it because it makes me feel good for a while. It gives me a sense of sweetness, although then it makes me tired.

It also has a downside: it gives me headaches and makes me sad—classic sugar crash. I could give you a technical rundown of what happens with the insulin overload and blood-sugar roller coaster, but you can get that in other books. (Hell, if you eat sugar the way I do—which, if you have any kind of substance addiction, the studies say you probably already have—you already know all about it from experience.)

I eat sugar because it does all kinds of things drugs do. It increases dopamine the way cocaine does and stimulates the mu opioid receptors in the same way heroin or any other opioid does, albeit more mildly. A 2008 Princeton University review of the literature showed there is strong evidence that sugar is an addictive substance. When I first read this study, my deep affinity for sterling rock-my-world pharma-grade opioid drugs made real sense to me for the first time in my life. Like my favorite drugs, sugar makes me energized, happy, and super-clear at first; then later it gently rocks me to sleep. It might even kill pain for a while. Certain kinds of pain.

Plus—and this is important—it tastes sweet. Other tastes that the tongue senses—bitter, sour, salty—are limited in their ability to trigger responses in the brain's reward centers, but sweet is not. We can keep eating sugary foods, and the sugar will keep triggering release of dopamine in the brain. "In this way, sugar acts a little bit like a drug," says Nicole Avena, Ph.D., a Princeton research neuroscientist, lead author of the study I mentioned, and an expert in nutrition and addiction. "It's one reason people seem to be hooked on sugary foods."

Sugar lends many of us—at high interest—the sweetness that we missed early in our lives. Instead of deriving a deep sense of security from a safe, loving home, I learned to distract myself, to make myself feel better by Taking Something—eating what there was to eat. I ate Cap'n Crunch, Lucky Charms, Count Chocula, any cereal that turned the milk a different color—and without fresh fruit (we only ever had apples and pears in the house, neither of which go with milk). I ate PB&J sandwiches made with Jif (60 percent sugar?!) and Wonder Bread, plus a Twinkie packed into my lunch box. After school, I ate another "goodie" from the cupboard. So, when I was a kid, my diet was at least 80 percent refined and processed food, and almost all of that, essentially, was sugar.

At age ten, I looked forward to my after-school snack the way my dad looked forward to his first beer when he got home. He would set his brief-case down in the corner by the piano, loosen his tie, and open the fridge. Dad's childhood indulgence in eating penny candy had primed him for alcoholism. In fact, beer metabolizes as sugar. According to studies and experts cited in *Eating Right to Live Sober*—one of the earliest popu-lar books about alcoholism and perhaps the first to mention the critical importance of nutrition in recovery—erratic processing of sugar result-ing in chronic low blood sugar is thought to underlie alcoholism. Like a candy bar, a shot of booze will provide an instant jolt of energy that soothes the restless, irritable, and discontented feelings caused by low blood sugar, which doctors call hypoglycemia. The problem is that alco-hol almost instantly converts into sugar, and the sugar drives insulin lev-els up, which makes blood-sugar levels crash, bringing on another bout of hypoglycemia—which then calls for another drink.

Rinse and repeat, and you can eventually get alcoholism.

Arielle, twenty-four, a New York City native who got sober during college and now lives in Seattle, grew up with parents who were dancers and personal trainers. Her mother, an acupuncturist in Manhattan, "is crazy with eating really right and exercising every day," she says. "I grew up with really good wholesome food—all organic and whole grains. Then I started drinking, and I ate like shit."

When Arielle got sober, she noticed that she craved sugar, and her mother told her that bingeing on refined sugar would simply replace the sugar-as-alcohol she'd given up in sobriety. "I used to have tubs of icing—I sometimes still do this; I could eat half a tub of icing in a sitting and be pretty happy about that," Arielle says. I love the way Arielle phrases her feelings. She doesn't assume that, just because you (or I) might feel like a piece of shit for eating half a tub of icing at one sitting, she has to feel like a piece of shit because she did this ~~unconscionable self-indulgent~~ fallible human thing. Which gives me permission for it not to make me feel like a piece of shit. Because, in fact, I have done this: I used to sit in the back of my senior-year advanced-placement English class and scoop out a big dollop of chocolate icing from a tub with my finger before passing it around to my girlfriends, and we all felt like shit about ourselves. I've eaten bags of cookies and multiple chocolate bars at a time, I've squeezed Hershey's syrup into my mouth from the economy-size bottle in the fridge door, and I've eaten my own raw cookie dough, which is so amazing that as I write this the mere thought makes my mouth water. And the worst part about all of that bingeing is not the gross sensual self-indulgence but the self-excoriation I enact upon myself afterward. "Excoriation" has the same root meaning as "sarcasm": the former means to rip the skin off, the latter means to tear the flesh away, and both habits are endemic in alcoholic family structures.

The antidote is lightness and humor—personified in Arielle. I had heard Arielle's "qualification" on the first anniversary of her sobriety. I had watched her come into recovery and metamorphose from the awkward, fumbling, caterpillarish creature each of us is in early recovery into a lithe, fit, happy young woman who could begin, in youth, to get down to the business of finding out who she is. Her refusal to judge herself for her behavior gives me permission not to judge myself. Of course, judging myself and understanding that I am loading my body with poison are two different actions, and this is what I appreciate about Arielle's level of self-acceptance: it shows she refuses to let her human struggles stand as proof that she's a bad person. Like me, she has renounced sugar, gone back to it, and given it up again. She knows returning to sugar is a sign that she is, as she says, "eating poorly to stifle reality." She understands that she obsesses about sugar. "Either I'm super stressed out, not dealing with emotional stuff," she says, "or I haven't been to a meeting in a while and haven't checked in with my sponsor. It's a sign that I need to hit a meeting and get back into my recovery work."

"My form of junk food was a lot of pizza, bread, bagels," says Phil, fifty, a New York City native who has been in recovery for thirteen years. "I was never two hundred pounds overweight and eating Cheetos every night. I was never into McDonald's."

Fortunately, however, Phil grew up in New York City with a Cuban grandma who was a wizard in the kitchen and taught him to appreciate taste and texture in food. Some people find that cooking enjoyable food is a way to occupy the abundance of time they suddenly have when they get sober and are no longer spending hours each month standing in line at the liquor store. When Phil quit drinking and smoking pot, he says, "Suddenly I had all this time on my hands—I'm not sitting around stoned and going to the bar. Cooking was one of the first things I did to occupy my time. In the initial few months of just being stark raving sober, I was cooking up a storm. I had no friends or lovers—I had isolated myself for the previous five years—so I was making four-course dinners for myself just to have something to do."

The night before our conversation, Phil says, he made a cilantro soup with monkfish, and shrimp tempura covered with a creamy chili garlic egg sauce. "That's a typical Saturday night at our house," he says. "It was dynamite!"

Like many people in recovery with whom I spoke, Phil doesn't follow any particular diet or nutritional plan. "My instinct was to take care of myself—not just quit the addictive stuff, but go back to good habits I'd had throughout my life," he says. His personal guidelines are, above all, to avoid processed foods and keep "white carbs"—bread, pasta, rice—to a minimum. Most of his carbs come from green vegetables, against which he balances meats. His breakfast, he says, is almost always the same every day: an egg-white omelet made with spinach and some sort of Asian sauce.

"As opposed to eating a few big meals, I try to eat more small meals throughout the day to keep my metabolism high," he says. "I think of my body as a fire—if I keep putting twigs on it, it continues to burn efficiently, but if I put a log on, it takes a long time for that one log to burn."

Rather than having a conversation with his body, Phil eats more as a routine, just like his meeting schedule, he says. "I don't process it through too much choice. Wednesday night I'm gonna go to my home group—there has to be a really good reason not to do that. I don't get into a lot of dialogue with myself about it. I handle my exercise and diet regimen the same—if I hear the part of me that says I don't want to, I push that aside as fast as I can. I'm doing breakfast because it's what I do. I'm going to a meeting because it's what I do."

Phil's nutrition habits suit his body. He has found the kinds of foods and the routine that keeps his blood sugar steady and his moods and energy levels even. My friend Lauri Lang, a registered dietitian and licensed dietitian nutritionist, emphasizes that it's important for people recovering from addiction to focus on regularity in eating and exercise. Her expertise validates my own experience. In early recovery, if I went more than four or five hours without eating, my body felt desperate and wanted to eat sugar—or else use a drug (whether caffeine or Vicodin) to boost my energy. Using a drug—Taking Something—had long been my solution.

"If you allow four to five hours to go by and you're not eating in that time frame, your body can experience hunger as withdrawal symptoms," Lauri says. She notes what so many nutrition books on the market are saying these days—that whole foods, especially a balance of protein, vegetables, and healthful fats, keep the body's blood sugar steady longer than starchy or sugary carbs.

Now in her mid-fifties, Lauri has two years sober from drinking and using drugs since she was thirteen, and although she never had a sweet tooth, after she got sober she found herself craving sugar. "I never liked shitty processed food, but since getting sober, I'll go buy three big cookies," she says. "Even the Big Book says we're supposed to eat candy. We eat donuts."

She's finding—and it's kind of ironic since she herself is a nutritionist—that paying attention to her food constitutes one of the most basic and generous acts of self-care in her days. "Whether you're an alcoholic or a drug addict, you're going to be malnourished, and the whole process of recovering the body is about replenishing the nutrient stores," she says. "This is where the commercial guidelines for RDA [recommended daily allowances] fall short. It's a difference between what you need so you're simply not deficient, and what your body needs to thrive. In the recovery process, hopefully a lot of us are focused on thriving."

Some folks, such as Phil, prefer to get all their vitamins from food. "I don't believe in supplements," he says. "If I were vegetarian or vegan, I'd take [vitamin] B12—that's the only one I'd take, but you can get that from cured meats like salami or sausage." Lauri recommends B-vitamin supplements, especially B12, which is critical to cognitive function and nerve health. "B vitamins and magnesium are cofactors in every reaction to unlock energy in our bodies," she says. "Alcohol rips through thiamine [vitamin B1] in particular—that's the whole cause of wet brain. Alcohol is *so toxic* to the digestive tract."

To detox the body effectively, she also recommends eliminating all food dyes.

"Instead of being preoccupied just with *How am I gonna keep this stream of my drug of choice at hand?* I plan how to create a new life of healing and recovery, caring for my body," she says. "To do that, I need vegetables and fruits and good protein in small meals every three to four hours. That way, our focus on self-care and comfort go together with recovery."

An "appetite" is a desire to satisfy a bodily need, especially for food. The word's Latin roots mean "to seek after," and the physical manifestation of appetite is hunger: a growling stomach, even some cramping, a salivating tongue, and heightened sense of taste and smell. The painkillers I took suppressed my appetite so that I never felt hungry, and they denied me the ordinary signs of appetite, which in healthy people can feel pleasurable. My stomach never growled, my mouth never watered, my body never felt as though it wanted to look for food—except, of course, for sugar.

By the time I hauled my body into detox, I was feeding it mostly sugar and, as Lauri says, "shitty processed food." Because the drugs threw my sleep cycles out of whack, in the mornings, I'd drag my body awake with a cup of strong tea with milk and sugar, and I'd down this with either a piece of toast with butter and jam or a chocolate protein bar that was a candy bar in disguise. This commercial ruse meshed perfectly with my level of addictive denial: protein bars were "health foods" sold in the "health and beauty" aisle of Whole Foods. Never mind that the label's list of ingredients (which I tried to ignore) said the bars were made of chocolate-candy-covered "soy protein isolate"—basically refined, processed soy pellets.

Eeww, right? But having grown up peeling Twinkies from their plastic wrapping, I could rationalize eating protein bars as a real step-up nutritionally. Tea and toast or a protein bar would be my breakfast, and I'd often skip lunch or snack on toast with Nutella spread—*The Swiss eat Nutella, and in Italy it's practically the national food!* I'd essentially regressed back to high school, except this time I wasn't sharing the tub of icing, I was keeping it all to myself.

Kids who grow up playing sports learn that eating food stokes their bodies with energy that fuels their physical activity. But despite being a die-hard Steelers fan who never missed a game on TV, my mother believed that school athletics were for "dumb jocks," and she wanted her kids to be smart, so she never encouraged us to go out for sports. Because as a kid I never kept my body active, I learned that eating was a matter not of fueling the body but of tasting something good and of alleviating feelings of fear and anger that I didn't know how to negotiate. Later, starving my appetites protected my self-worth, which was grounded in physical appearances and academic performance. Painkillers not only helped me with my starvation-and-beautification project, but they also gave me a kick of energy that felt almost but not quite like the energy I got from food. As a matter of fact, the painkillers' kick was even better than food energy (technically known as "calories") because food—and alcohol—would make me fat, but drugs wouldn't.

Drugs were calorie-free: *Vicodin Zero.*

I've come to think of this solution as "fake energy." The boost lasted a few hours, and while I checked everything off my agenda, the drugs tapped out my adrenal glands and the rest of my endocrine system. I was running on empty from coast to coast.

Later in the day, I'd desultorily make dinner for my family, and I'd set it on the table, but I'd rarely be able to eat. By the end of my active addiction, I was constantly in some level of withdrawal, or fear of withdrawal—or just fear—and I could not sit my body still on a chair for ten minutes at a time. The constant chemical hijacking that the drugs were pulling off inside my body—the continual Taking Something—left no room for *eating* anything, and my weight dwindled to 115 pounds, sometimes less. My addiction starved my body into the picture I described at the beginning of this book—the skinny, sallow woman whose heroin-chic hipbones stuck out and whose haunted eyes were ringed with brown circles. My ransacked body was weak and deprived of stamina.

But hey: I was thin! Small.

If I stayed small—in so many ways—I could fly under the radar. I wouldn't need to cry or laugh. I wouldn't run the risk of activating any appetites—food wouldn't appeal to me; men wouldn't appeal to me; hell, my own body wouldn't even appeal to me. I wouldn't have to know anybody, starting with myself. I wouldn't have to take those risks. I wouldn't have to feel my own strength and power pushing against the depth of life's danger and, out of necessity, creating something useful and beautiful. And with the numbing of these dangerous feelings came the renunciation of joy and pleasure. Because food no longer tasted pleasurable, I no longer ate much. I could use my drugs and capture a fleeting feeling of satisfaction in the escalation of my numbness, my triumph over the rules and regulations of doctors and pharmacies and of anatomy and physiology, my absolute domination over my appetites and physical drives. I could pretend I had no needs, desires, preferences. I could remain trapped inside my own self-consciousness, inside the small, round walls of my skull.

I could live alone—while moving among others, entirely alone.

But I belong to *Homo sapiens*—that's the tribe into which I was born. And the individuals in my tribe, however diverse they may be, are not evolved to live alone. We just cannot sustain that life for long, or the structure of life breaks down and the delusions take over. Addiction creates an unsustainable life. And life that's unsustainable is headed toward ruin.

A good friend of mine put together several years sober, then relapsed on one five-milligram Percocet. What led to her relapse? Weeks of compulsive use of Sudafed, a.k.a. pseudoephedrine, an over-the-counter amphetamine, a.k.a. speed. My friend had gotten sober off crystal meth (a.k.a. überspeed), plus heroin, plus kratom, which is a southeast Asian herb that activates the mu opioid receptors. (She spent a fortune in the mid-2000s ordering kratom from rainforest distributors, delivered via FedEx.) Then, like me, she detoxed using Suboxone. She put together a couple years, but then started taking Sudafed for a head cold, she said. And she remembered how much she enjoyed the fact that over-the-counter speed killed her appetites. She dropped ten pounds right away, which plunged her into the varicose vanity (a.k.a. distortion of truth, a.k.a. delusion) inherent in the illness of addiction: *If everything looks cool, then Everything Is Cool.*

This is the same delusion that drives some of us to diet, run triathlon after marathon, bench-press bigger and bigger barbells—while also eating donuts and smoking cigarettes: *If only I could look cool, then I Would Be Cool.* In recovery, we have to guard against addiction's propensity to make us focus on the superficiality of appearances and overlook deeper health concerns, such as chronically high blood pressure, unstable hormone responses, cardiopulmonary stress, cardiovascular dysfunction, and other problems.

"In a period of my life when I was, like, chemically sober but exercising too much, definitely several nights a week I could binge on ice cream but tell myself it would be okay because I would work out," says Matthew, a thirty-three-year-old financial analyst and former bodybuilder who has been in and out of recovery since 2006 and has most recently been sober since the beginning of 2014. "I'd buy two pints of Ben & Jerry's, knowing full well that I'd eat both pints before bed. I have a problem with dairy—ice cream and sweets. I hated when people told me those cravings passed—but it's true they do."

It makes me feel so much better to hear Matthew confess his sugar binges that I can't possibly express my relief while I'm actually talking to him, and I am, for once, speechless. To hear a ripped young dude admit that he has binged on sweets, that he has eaten two pints of Ben & Jerry's ice cream before bed, rationalizing that he can just "burn it off"? Most awesome. What I want to do is thank Matthew on behalf of all the women who might read this and feel so fucking relieved that, in our under-the-covers worship of Cherry Garcia and Phish Food, we are not alone—not just among women but also among the other testosterone-loaded half of humanity.

It's a fallacy that we can just eat addictively and burn away our overindulgence through compulsive exercise. It's common for folks who exercise a lot to reward themselves with cookies or ice cream, but a small but growing body of research indicates that extreme exercise may actually aggravate cardiovascular problems and contribute to atherosclerosis, or a build-up of plaque inside the arteries.

Matthew says he tries not to obsess about food. "Drawing those hard lines in the sand about what I can and can't eat just makes me think about them more, and then I feel worse when I can't meet them," he says.

Matthew's experience illustrates what research shows, that eating well and taking care of our appetites in recovery is just as difficult a job for men as it is for women. A 2008 Cornell University study of men's eating habits in recovery published in the journal *Appetite* turned up several interesting findings. During active addiction, drugs release dopamine, and this makes men not want to eat. Then, in recovery, when dopamine finally stabilizes and hunger comes roaring back, men tend to overindulge their appetites and gain back too much weight. And the men's overeating wasn't caused only by their bodies' need to compensate for the malnutrition of active addiction. The men in recovery particularly craved sweets. This study and others have found that addicts in the first six months of recovery use sweet foods and refined, processed foods—junk food—to satisfy cravings for drugs and alcohol. The authors pointed out that sensible eating habits are seldom part of recovery strategies in detox and rehab facilities—this was a concern echoed by a number of treatment experts I talked with.

"Most of the participants in this study lacked from the start and did not gain during recovery the necessary nutrition skills to move forward into healthy eating," the authors wrote.

"More than 50 percent of my clients are women, but I have a number of male clients too. They often have problems with addiction, and they often say things like, 'Once I start eating sugar, I can't stop,'" says Jenna Hollenstein, a thirty-eight-year-old dietitian and nutritionist based in New York City who runs a nutrition therapy practice called Eat to Love. Hollenstein's nondiet, "intuitive-eating" orientation toward her therapy is designed, she says, to help clients "redefine fullness"—a play on words. In this context the word "fullness" can also mean "fulfillment" or "satisfaction," even "contentment," a more emotional sensation than just the physical feeling of eating until one's belly is no longer empty. Hollenstein says she thinks of her practice as teaching clients to eat while "tolerating a full range of feelings."

"My god," I say, mentally counting the ways I've binged on chocolate to escape feelings of anger or terror, "if I could manage that, I'd be so happy."

"You *can* manage that," she says. "You're fine just the way you are—all the messiness—that's all great."

Hollenstein quit drinking on her thirty-third birthday more than six years ago and has stayed sober through a practice of meditation and awareness of the foods and substances she puts into her body. I realized while talking with Hollenstein that I felt reluctant to explore with her the subjects of eating and drinking—it was hard not to lapse into my obsession with appearances—because she is such a classical beauty: she has fair skin, dark eyes and long dark hair, dimples framing a perfect smile, a beautiful figure. Hollenstein is ten years younger than I am, which means she's not quite forty. So she's still what Americans might call "young," and I put the question to her bluntly: "I ask this as a woman who has been told she's beautiful and that she looks fifteen years younger than she is— but you're *truly* gorgeous, right? And don't you think it's easy to tell me, 'You're fine just the way you are,' when you actually *do* meet all the criteria the world puts on us and you don't 'need' to starve yourself?"

"I don't know, because I don't see myself the way other people see me," she says slowly, and the deliberation of her answer and its meaning point the way toward a solution for addicts' fucked-up handling of food: a relationship with oneself and one's body. "The way I relate to myself is not necessarily the way other people *think* I relate to myself, or to the world," she says. "And how many stories do you hear of people who seem to have it all and who are miserable, for one reason or another?"

Some of Hollenstein's clients indeed "have it all," which is to say they have high-powered and high-paying jobs that allow them to live in nice apartments, houses, and vacation homes. They're citizens of the globe. And it's just these trappings—the titles, addresses, clothing, cars, devices, delicious food—that distract them from their lives, from the people they care about, starting with themselves. The emphasis on eating in this society,

Hollenstein says, is often on "weight loss," on numbers on scales and im-ages in mirrors rather than on behaviors, thoughts, and feelings that drive us to eat when we're not physically hungry.

"I see these people on Facebook and on other sites posting pictures of their abs: they went from 325 pounds to 125, and now they want to tell everybody," she says. "They're deriving their self-worth from their six-pack. On the outside, they look like they've got it figured out. But on the inside—what about when they're sixty, and they're not gonna have the same six-pack that they had when they were thirty? Where does their self-worth come from then?"

I mention a book I saw in Whole Foods that promised to teach sugar-addicted readers how to detox from sugar, and with every sensible piece of nutritional advice (eat whole foods, eat protein and organic vegetables, stay away from processed food) comes the promise that readers will not only feel stronger and more healthy but they will also Look Younger.

"If someone is quitting drugs or alcohol, chances are their skin *is* going to look different," Hollenstein says. "That's one of the first things I noticed—within three weeks of quitting alcohol, my skin looked better. If you're removing refined and processed sugars from your diet, and if they previously made up 30 percent of your diet or more, you probably will no-tice physical changes. For example, you might retain less water."

But the idea that there's a promise of looking younger woven through-out an otherwise healthful plan of eating sounds confusing, she says. "Why do we *have* to look younger? Who are we looking younger *for?* In gen-eral, we eat too much sugar, and I think we don't even realize how much we're taking in. That said, I don't know that people need to do something quite so restrictive" as cutting out all fruit and dairy, as this book recom-mended. "I think these diets—'eating green and clean'—become a weird fixation. It's like an addiction in its own right: *'Oh—that's the thing that's gonna fix me.'*"

Instead of counting calories and keeping exercise journals, Hollenstein teaches her clients to settle back into their bodies and hold a conversa-tion when they feel cravings for particular foods. "I had one client who claimed he couldn't stop once he started eating sugar. He noticed so many things about his body and his experience by slowing down. And this is a very high-level businessman who's traveling all over the world, who's always at business dinners," she says. "By slowing things down, he was able to take a step back and realize that many times he was choosing to eat not out of physical hunger—and he was able to be in touch with what he needs at those times. *Even if he can't give it to himself,*" she emphasizes. "Because in some cases he might realize, 'You know what? I might just need to take a break, even though I'm in the middle of a meeting and can't take one right now. What I don't need is another handful of M&Ms.'"

I ask her to break down the idea of "slowing down" while dealing with a desire to eat. She asks her clients to focus on their physical sensations of hunger—of becoming intimate with their appetites, of chatting with their bodies about a craving, of putting language to a desire for sensory properties of foods that contain high levels of sugar: *creamy, dense, chewy.* "A lot of times the foods that contain a lot of sugar have a texture or sensory property that also gives comfort," she says.

Instead of stifling our body's desires either by starving it or by indulging in compulsive eating, we can slow down, return to the body, and hold conversations like this. And we might find out some surprising facts about what our bodies really want.

"I've had clients say, when they are asked to smell, and look at, then feel, then eat a single M&M, that it's a very different experience from when they take a handful of M&Ms and shove it in their mouths," Hollenstein says. "And sometimes they realize they don't even really like M&Ms, you know? When you take a handful of M&Ms and shove it in your mouth, there's a chemical reaction that just overrides your ability to be mindful. And when you consciously slow down that experience—*How does this feel in my mouth? What does this taste like? Is it the way I expected it to taste? Is this actually even what I wanted?*—then mindfulness interrupts our fixation.

"I'm not expecting people to become totally mindful eaters who are completely connected to the moment from the time they take the first bite to the time they take the last bite," she says. "That's not realistic. But it's sort of like working out a muscle. What I try to get people to do, even if it's only for a moment each day, is to interrupt the mindless activity by asking themselves the questions, 'What am I feeling in this moment, and what do I need?' Even without the expectation of being able to answer these questions, you get closer to the truth. Because if you ask the questions enough—if you *trust* yourself enough to ask them—eventually a curiosity develops that is separate from that story we tell ourselves that 'I'm feeling lonely—I *need* these M&Ms.'"

The ability to hold a conversation with the body's appetites reduces overwhelming feelings and has the power to teach us what is enough.

I know a chef who got sober several years ago who says he never ate sugar before he quit drugs and booze. As a chef, he works late hours and, of course, after work he used to drink. "Now that I'm sober, I'll come home after work and go into the kitchen, grab a piece of bread, load it with peanut butter, then pour a bunch of Hershey's syrup on top," he says. "It's like a big Reese's peanut butter cup!" He cackles at himself: he knows his little culinary creation is nauseating, makes him risk putting on weight, and offends his well-honed aesthetic sense of What Good Food Is. There's nothing about this "sandwich" that he wants except the sugar hit. And like most of us in recovery, he does it anyway. "Addiction," Philip Seymour Hoffman reportedly told a friend, "is when you do the thing you really, really most don't want to be doing."

Yes: the root of the word "addict" is the Latin term for "enslave."

Coincidentally my chef pal and I were having this little chat in front of the Whole Foods salad bar, where I was picking up my dinner. I'd found him scouting out the huge chafing pans of food at the hot bar, where all the busy professionals were grazing after work. I said, "How can you stand eating this stuff?" Like some master cooks I've known, he doesn't make lavish meals for himself. He likes simple things, he says. Another chef I know who has six years clean from heroin once told me he likes nothing better than a dinner of roast pork and mashed potatoes.

As for me, I often loathe cooking, the way I loathe washing and ironing clothes and scrubbing toilets. I started cooking for my entire family when I was ten, and by the time I was my son's age—sixteen, a junior in high school, earning all As in the advanced courses, editing the newspaper, designing theatrical sets, playing first-chair flute, an ass-busting high achiever—I was coming home after school to starch, iron, and fold my father's shirts and clean the bathroom on Saturdays, and one or two nights a week I made dinner for everyone. My mother was a truly abysmal cook, and in adulthood I learned to improve my skills with cookbooks, but the pleasure of creating good food, of experimenting with tastes and textures—"the joy of cooking," as it were—was quashed early by the requirement that I take care of others at my own expense. As a teenager, I had precious little time and, with chronic migraines, even less physical energy to be cooking for five people after school, but I did it to earn my mother's approval. When my mother approved of me, it was as though the sun might shine on my face for all eternity. In adulthood I have often thought that if I could eat out for the rest of my life—or more desirable but less likely, have someone who cares about me cook good food for me—it would be like finding a glass slipper that fit my size-nine foot.

Like most of the world's people, though, I've had to learn how to make the food that my body needs to thrive. Because I've had such a complicated relationship with food, especially the drug of refined carbohydrates, I've explored all kinds of diets: Barry Sears' Zone diet, Sandra Cabot's Liver Cleansing Diet, Bob Greene's Best Life diet. While I was doing P90X, I was eating the recommended Fat Shredder diet, despite the fact that, at five-feet-five and 120 pounds, I didn't have any fat to shred. The Paleo diet, which I haven't tried, takes aim at grains and says *Homo sapiens* is not "wired" to eat cookies, cakes, pizza, or even bread, which my father, a bread-eating Croatian to his last cell, was fond of calling "the staff of life."

(I love it when people talk about human beings as though we were robots. Last time I checked, my heart and central nervous system—which are chock-full of electrical circuits, with energy cells that can be recharged *ad infinitum*—contained no "wires." My body may be "evolved" for some functions, but I am not "wired" for anything.)

Dr. David Perlmutter, author of the blockbuster book *Grain Brain: The Surprising Truth about Wheat, Carbs, and Sugar—Your Brain's Silent Killers,* advocates an entirely gluten-free diet to reduce inflammation, which he somewhat controversially cites as a risk for many illnesses, including Alzheimer disease and other dementia, ADHD, depression, anxiety—and migraines.

Books like Perlmutter's may have much truth in them, but by vilifying one dietary ingredient, they essentially promise a panacea: *Just nix this one food and you will live longer, feel stronger, look awesome, totally avoid dementia—you will Be Fixed*. ("There's either a scapegoat or a silver bullet in almost every best-selling diet book," said Dr. David Katz, founding director of Yale University's Prevention Research Center and author of two editions of a clinical nutrition textbook, in an interview about Perlmutter's *Grain Brain* in *The Atlantic* magazine.) We all want the perfect fix. I have often thought, while standing for backbreaking hours in bookstore aisles, that if I could just find the right diet, maybe my headaches would disappear, the knots in my shoulders and back would unclasp, I would feel rested, Life Would Be Perfect. *There must be a diet to fix me.*

There are so many books and plans out there that contain at least some sound nutritional advice, complete with menus to tell us what to eat and even how to cook it. The best ones rehash in well-photographed detail the conclusions Michael Pollan presents most elegantly in his book *Food Rules: An Eater's Manual*:

> Eat food,
>
> not too much,
>
> mostly plants.

And for a while I'd succeed in following these recipes. I'd put a picture of Rachael Ray's *Express Lane Meals'* "cheat sheet for all the go-to basics" in my phone so I'd know what to buy at the grocery store ("capers, bread crumbs, EVOO"). But eventually, because I'd be cooking for three different preferences—a grown man with sophisticated tastes in Indian, Mexican, and Thai; a teenager who likes steak and mac and cheese; and me—I'd give up. I realized these books' attractiveness lies not in their ability to help me think for myself about what my body wants to eat and to help me plan it, but in their sumptuously art-directed photographs of colorful dishes, their *#foodporn*: one of the most popular hashtags on Instagram. Everyone loves *looking* at good food, but not many of us—at least, I often don't—want to invest the time and money it takes to make it.

Especially because, at 4:30 p.m., that witching time when people around the world have to begin contemplating what to make for dinner, I no longer have drugs to get me through the tedium of wading through the grocery store, hauling home the catch, and cooking it. Instead, I've had to learn to use my own mind and stamina to slog through the daily decision of How And What To Eat. David Foster Wallace told the graduates of Kenyon College in 2005, in his marvelous commencement address that was later reprinted as the book *This Is Water*,

> But if you really learn how to pay attention, . . . then . . . [i]t will actually be within your power to experience a crowded, hot, slow, consumer-hell-type situation as not only meaningful, but sacred, on fire with the same force that made the stars: love, fellowship, the mystical oneness of all things deep down.

I learned how to pay that kind of attention while in the middle of writing this book. Sometimes (all the time, actually; it's a lie that it's only *sometimes*) we can't separate professional life from Real Life, from the life of parenting and marriage and friendships and housecleaning and the soul-killing consumer hell of modern grocery shopping, and that was true of me last year. While deep in research for this book, I hit the holidays: Thanksgiving, Christmas, the New Year. I also hit a hormonal traffic jam. Women my age, which happens at this moment to be forty-nine, usually experience what my mother called "The Change of Life" and what today is medically called "menopause."

"Your grandmother had a difficult time with The Change of Life," my mother always told me, although I don't remember the details, if she ever confided them, of Grandma's difficulties. My mother herself, at about my age, had grapefruit-sized fibroid tumors that led her to have a hysterectomy. A difficult time with menopause seems, along with addiction, to be front-loaded into my genes, because "difficulty" is putting it mildly for what I experienced: inordinate bleeding that led to anemia that required multiple transfusions. In the middle of writing this book, I had to have surgery to stop the bleeding—the third such surgery in two years— followed by another transfusion. And I was severely advised (by doctors who looked like they were in high school with my son and who seemed weary of dealing with yet another cranky older "lady" who was afraid she was bleeding to death) that the transfusions were only a "temporizing measure," that I would have to seriously consider "surgery" because my little bean-sized two-centimeter fibroid had grown into a five-centimeter tumor, a two-inch golf ball invading the wall of my uterus and making my body bleed.

By "surgery," of course, they meant "hysterectomy." Which, when I heard that word, I didn't hear a tidy little "operation." I heard this: "We're gonna cut out your uterus."

"What about changing the way I eat?" I said, thinking about the piles of sugar I'd eaten addictively over the holidays: cookies, candy, pies, my friend Petra's daughter Ella's muffins and scones and excellent "monkey bread," drizzled with cinnamon-and-sugar glaze. I myself had made several strudels—from scratch!—according to Grandma's recipe and served them hot, with vanilla ice cream.

I should have expected their answer.

"What you eat won't make any difference," the sixteen-year-old doctors said, and I felt condemned to a hysterectomy.

"Why don't you just *get rid of that thing*?" some women asked me.

"I know a doctor who can take that thing out and have you back at your desk within forty-eight hours," another gynecologist, this one my age, told me with utter confidence.

What? Slice out my uterus? *That thing,* that lovely estrogen-and-testosterone-sensitive organ of procreation and pleasure. The dark, warm, wet home where my son kicked and floated for nine months before worming his slow way into the dry, cold, blinding planetary atmosphere. The smooth, fist-sized muscle that swells with blood when I'm touched in my hot core, then contracts in rhythms that beat with stone-age war-cries, with Cuban rumbas, Brazilian sambas?

I don't *think* so.

"I don't blame you for wanting to save your uterus," a friend of mine, a pelvic reconstructive surgeon who's about my age, said when I called her for advice. She noted that a hysterectomy would change the entire architecture of my pelvis: with the absence of the uterus, organs would shift and the large intestine would be pushed against the bladder, creating a potentially dangerous compression. Plus, it can't be denied that some women, myself included, experience uterine orgasm: the contractions throb throughout my belly, creating pleasure in my entire pelvis (more about this—*lucky you!*—in chapter 5).

No sir, I ain't givin' that up without a fight.

I remembered reading French physician David Servan-Schreiber's descriptions of refined sugar feeding cancer tumors, and I wondered whether sugar also fed fibroids. The doctors had all told me my body was either making or being exposed to too much estrogen, which makes fibroids grow and can cause heavy bleeding. It turns out that eating excessive amounts of refined sugar and starches can promote higher estrogen levels. Refined sugar and flours also slow down the gut and wreak havoc with intestinal flora, and eating too much of them can lead to a fatty liver, all of which prevent the body from efficient elimination of estrogen.

I read scores of statements from women on a variety of websites saying it was possible to stop fibroids from bleeding by cutting out sugar and caffeine and by increasing intake of vitamins A and D, specifically through fermented fish oil. Also recommended for my problem: an ounce or two of raw, fermented apple cider vinegar each day to improve liver function. And effective negotiation of stress.

I was skeptical. There's no "science" behind these "home remedies," only what researchers call "anecdotal evidence"—tons of real-life experience of women who did not want their bodies cut open. And I couldn't imagine asking a physician to help me verify whether cod liver oil could be a next step in medical treatment.

I sat alone in a darkened room in the women's hospital emergency room, two units of graciously donated type O-negative red blood cells trickling into my arm, my computer open on my lap, women's stories about their fibroids speaking to me from all over the world. I decided that, yes, my body was worth taking care of, my uterus was well worth working to save. If there were a chance of keeping it by giving up sugar and caffeine, I'd go to those lengths, however extreme they felt. The next day at my food co-op I bought a bottle of unflavored fermented cod liver oil, scooped out a grim heaping teaspoonful, knocked it back with a mouthful of lemonade to cut the grease in my throat. It was the beginnings of a daily first-thing-in-the-morning routine: unsweetened green tea, sprouted-grain toast with almond butter and raw honey, cod liver oil, apple cider vinegar to detoxify my liver and improve my digestion so my body, I hoped, could get rid of excess hormones.

Need I say this? I'm not prescribing this or any other regimen or formula for anyone, just telling you what I found worked for me *at this time in my life.* If there's a theme in this book, it's Find What Works for You—or as they say, "Take what you need and leave the rest."

Three days later, my bleeding stopped. The next month, I had a normal period.

I can hear the skeptics because a vocal one resides in my own mind: *Who knows whether all that stuff made the bleeding stop? Who knows how long her normal cycles will last? Who knows whether it was just a fluke?* Right. Nobody knows. Here's the way my recovery asks me to live now: A month from today I might have to have a hysterectomy. Next week my addiction might relapse. Today, though, I'm doing what seems to be working to avoid using drugs or having my body cut open to remove a vital organ.

It was only after my bleeding stopped that I realized the strength of my sugar habit. How powerfully sugar, when I take it into my body, acts like a drug. I don't believe the myth that says addicts necessarily need to "hit bottom" to be ready to get help, but I do believe that we humans have to take personal responsibility for our recovery from any illness, and it bothers me that, in order to take that responsibility, I seem to need some sort of gun held to my temple or an asp held to my breast. With drugs, the choice was prison, fatal overdose, or abstinence and recovery; with sugar, it was between indulgence in my oldest, most comforting chemical compulsion and preserving my physical and sexual integrity.

Because today's refined, packaged foods are scientifically engineered to taste good and keep us coming back for more—not to stoke our bodies with good fuel but to ensure our financial investment—many of us are finding ourselves in the same quite literal life-and-death situations. My friend Lucy, who has ten years sober and abstinent, texts me: "I am a perfect example of how healthy eating, exercise, and spiritual connection can make a person feel great—such a contrast to a couple of months ago." Lucy, fifty-five, is recovering from both addiction and thyroid cancer. Since her surgeon removed her thyroid eighteen months ago, she has struggled with hormonal imbalances that have slowed her metabolism while simultaneously inhibiting her appetite and making her body put on weight. For many months she couldn't feel hunger pangs—but at the same time, even when she restricted her calories, she packed on pounds, and it was a mortal effort to exercise. She just didn't have the energy. She thought something had to be amiss with her hormones. So she consulted a nutritionist, who ordered extensive hormone tests and discovered that Lucy has a high fasting insulin level, making her a prime candidate for metabolic disorder and diabetes if she doesn't make changes. The nutritionist recommended a change in Lucy's thyroid hormone supplementation, which kick-started her metabolism and helped her to begin losing the weight she'd put on.

"I found out I have an eating disorder; I don't just have a sugar addiction," she says. "I finally acknowledged that I have a bingeing problem." But *how* did she quit sugar? It's like asking a smoker *how* he quit nicotine. Asking a drug addict *how* she quit fentanyl.

"I realized that despite everything I'd done to my body, I deserve to take care of my body," she says. No matter what we ate or drank or used, that's what it comes down to: realizing we're worth the care and attention it takes not just to get through each day but to nourish the house in which we live. "My body *deserves* to be treated well," she says.

Which means it deserves to be fed well.

"I don't have that shit in the house," Lucy says of sugar and packaged foods. "And I don't bake. If you see me baking, things aren't good—that's my emotional response to stress. I can't bake, because then I eat the stuff I bake."

As for me, I still eat chocolate, but I buy small quantities, and it has to be very dark, more than 70 percent, with less than ten grams of sugar per serving. Lucy and I agreed that somehow more than ten grams of sugar activates our craving for the entire chocolate bar—or multiple chocolate bars. In addition, just as the registered dietitian Lauri emphasizes, good fats can help satisfy the body's appetites, and cocoa butter—a primary ingredient of extra-dark chocolate—is an excellent fat.

Eating according to my body's needs has taught me not just about the power of holding conversations with my body to promote my recovery but also about the strength of my resistance to doing what's good for me. About two weeks into my regimen of cod liver oil and apple cider vinegar, my bleeding and cramping had—miraculously, it seemed—ceased. Then one day I woke up and remembered: I've got to eat that damned stuff all over again. It's essentially the same thought I had the day I realized I had to quit drugs: *I can never Take Something again, I have to change, this has to last* forever—*I can't do it!*

If I think of it as "forever," I start counting the rivers of fish oil I'll have to swallow and the days of discomfort I have to drag through without Taking Something. But if, as Hollenstein and my friends in recovery suggest, I slow down, break the job into pieces, I can manage one day.

And rivers of fish oil in fact do not exist. One spoonful takes two seconds to swallow.

Some Guidelines

Here are some guidelines to follow as you begin, or continue, to nourish the permanent home that is your body:

- Avoid processed foods. Anything that can't go bad on the shelf is probably bad for our bodies.
- Avoid added sugar.
- Learn to cook with whole foods, especially vegetables and, if possible, grass-fed meats.
- Experiment with nutrition habits that suit your body.
- Option: Have a conversation with your body to learn what it really wants to eat.
- Option: Make your eating a routine, like your meeting schedule. For a while, eat the same things over and over so your body gets used to good food and you don't have to think about making choices.
- Instead of three large meals, eat five or six smaller plates to keep your blood sugar level steady.

- Consider a B-vitamin supplement.
- When you feel a desire to binge, slow down, settle back into the body, and ask your body what it needs.

Seeking Peace of Mind and Body
Sleep

· · · · · · ·

People say, "I'm going to sleep now," as if it were nothing.
But it's really a bizarre activity. "For the next several hours, while
the sun is gone, I'm going to become unconscious, temporarily losing
command over everything I know and understand. When the sun returns,
I will resume my life." If you didn't know what sleep was, and you had
only seen it in a science fiction movie, you would think it was weird
and tell all your friends about the movie you'd seen.

—George Carlin, *Brain Droppings*

Good sleep—"Sleep that knits up the raveled sleeve of care," as Shakespeare wrote in *Macbeth,* the story of a king whose self-delusion about his lousy marriage and acts of murder made him, among other things, an insomniac—is about more than just good "sleep hygiene." (As if there were a way to "sleep dirty"?) Sleep is a quintessential practice of surrender and acceptance of reality. With sleep, more than with exercise or nutrition, peace of mind plays a part in how well our bodies function—how well they can slip into (as the play's verse continues) the "balm of hurt minds," the "chief nourisher in life's feast."

One of my earliest memories is of my father trying to sing me to sleep. I was about four, so he must have been not yet thirty, and he was holding my little body draped over his broad shoulder while he walked up and down our upstairs hallway in the dark. My memory was that I was sick—with an ear infection? a stomach bug? I'll never know. Dad was a tall guy, six-feet-two, and I felt so high up in the air that, in my mind's eye, I might have been hanging from the ceiling lamp. But what has inscribed this scene indelibly in my mind is the song he sang to try to put me to sleep. I have no idea what made him pick "Go Tell Aunt Rhody," an old folk song about a goose that drowns in a millpond. Dad tried to sing it slowly, as a lullaby. But being blessed with a vivid imagination is sometimes a curse. Even at four, I could picture the old gray goose standing on her head in the cold, black water. With my dad's deep bass voice and all the imagery of death in the song, the song flipped me out, and I couldn't stop crying. My father shushed me, patting my back but carrying on droning his dirge.

It never occurred to me to ask him to pick another song.

A fundamental structure in families affected by addiction is an inability to be honest about our feelings. My mother was raised in a violent alcoholic family—her father regularly got drunk after work, kicked her younger brother, and wrecked the house before the neighbors called the cops—so she had learned it was too dangerous to tell the truth about how she felt. From as far back as I can remember, she imparted this to me, her eldest child and the one with whom she most closely identified. So instead of asking Daddy to stop singing about the dead duck, I did as I thought he wanted me to do: I lay still on his shoulder and tried to stop crying. But have you ever seen a frenzied kid try to stop her own hysterics? Her diaphragm spasms, she hitches and sniffs, and her lack of control over her own body freaks her out even more. For a long time this seemingly inconsequential scene gave me nightmares and reinforced my fear of my dad.

During my childhood and early adulthood, I had repeated bouts of insomnia, usually when the stress of academics, friendships, and family relationships became unmanageable. I never learned how to express my feelings and allow peace of mind to calm my body.

The inability to tell the truth about my feelings took an even greater toll on me after I had my son. All parents want their kids' lives to be better than their own, but with me this was a kind of pathological compulsion. I needed to save Jonathan from the kind of unhappiness I'd experienced when I was a kid.

Though I intermittently drank and overused prescription drugs before I had my son, in part the loss of sleep—driven by the loss of peace of mind—after he was born drove me right into the long tunnel of addiction. I gave birth to Jonathan in a thirty-one-hour labor that left my body banged up, exhausted, and vulnerable to the flu that was going around that fall. After childbirth, my sleep was compromised not just by physical pain but also by an irrational, uncontrollable fear of Jonathan's crying. He would cry, it was inevitable, but I didn't accept that. Despite everything the baby books and the experienced moms I knew said, I kept telling myself that his crying proved I was a lousy mother. As though everybody else's new baby was allowed to cry, but not mine. As though if I'd been able to be a "good mother," he would have stopped crying. Or rather, the other way around: as though if he'd been able to stop crying, it would have proved I was an awesome mother.

So as the weeks passed, he carried on being a normal baby, and I grew more irrationally afraid of him. And I couldn't figure this out: *How could I possibly be so afraid of my own kid?* Since then, I've talked with other mothers who were afraid of their kids—usually women who as young girls were raised to take responsibility for the feelings of other people, starting with their mothers. We "people pleasers" become terrified when other people cry and nothing we do or say makes it okay.

I tried like hell to put Jonathan to sleep by nursing him on demand, rocking him, singing to him, doing whatever I could to manage his stress. I must have walked him miles inside the house, holding him without the help of a sling—he hated the way slings forced him to fold his legs, so I held him the way he liked best, at the cost of my own strength. The harder I tried to take away all his unpleasant feelings, the more I may have imparted to his small body my own tension, frustration, and fear. Members of our species have finely tuned sensory perception. Infant *Homo sapiens* are like little sponges when it comes to their parents' feelings, and it's well documented that the more anxious the mother, the more anxious her baby. Interestingly, the practices that help new mothers reduce their anxiety are the same ones that help people with addiction recover their bodies, including regular exercise, good nutrition, avoiding drugs and alcohol, and finding community.

Eventually Jonathan and I found a rhythm that served him, but cost me. He'd cry, I'd get up and walk or nurse him, and he'd fall back to sleep. Then I'd lie awake at night, unable to close my eyes again. Because he cried every day and nothing I did stopped him—and because I had never learned how to give other people, even kids, the dignity of their own experiences—I slipped further and further into a delusion that provided an engine for my addiction, a trait commonly called "people-pleasing." I needed to Make Everyone Okay. I couldn't risk anyone's criticism or disapproval. Sticking to that impossible standard caused me enormous fear, which in turn cost me years of insomnia (which is just fear of sleep, of surrender), which I then managed with drugs.

In hindsight, and with some years of recovery behind me, it's easy to see the harsh self-judgment that underlay this aspect of my drug use. During those sleepless nights, I used to think I needed to find a way to "reduce my stress." It now really bugs me when people say "stress" causes addiction. It's not the stress that does it. Everybody's life includes stress. Even babies experience stress—it's a reality of human life, even before birth, and our bodies and minds have evolved exquisite mechanisms to handle it. But if we live in a fucked-up family that doesn't teach us those mechanisms, then we invent our own half-assed mechanisms. Trying to reinvent the wheel is never an effective strategy.

What drives addiction is not "stress" but the unsustainable ways we negotiate stress. As a child I learned that trying to make my mother okay (and later my friends, and later my husband, and later my kid) was the only way I could feel any peace and experience even a fleeting moment of rest in my mind and body. So historically, when stress has hit, I have started scrambling to fix the problems and feelings of everyone around me.

My participation in this huge delusion—a legacy of my addictive family—promises me peace of mind with one hand and, with the other, robs me of it and sabotages my ability to sleep.

Today, in order to sleep, I try to tell myself the truth, then I try to tell other people the truth. I practice peace of mind.

Physiologically speaking, the sleep picture in active addiction is pretty simple. There are those of us (the meth users, the cokeheads and crack-heads, people who pop prescription amphetamines) who could never get to sleep; then there are those of us (the drunks, the potheads, the opioid junkies) who nodded or passed out and couldn't stay awake. According to studies by the National Sleep Foundation, almost 20 percent of adults have used alcohol to help themselves sleep, a figure that has roughly been matched by several other studies. Among those in addiction treatment that percentage more than doubles, according to other research, and insomnia is a reliable indicator of potential relapse. In other words, if we don't learn to take care of our ability to sleep, we run the risk of relapsing.

Unresolved sleep problems in early childhood may predict substance use later in life to manage stress. A 2004 University of Michigan study showed that sleep problems in kids ages three to five significantly pre-dicted use of alcohol, cannabis, drugs, and nicotine by ages twelve to fourteen. "This is, to our knowledge, the first study that prospectively examines the relationship between sleep problems and early onset of alco-hol use, a marker of increased risk for later alcohol problems and alcohol use disorders," the authors wrote. So teaching our kids skills for promot-ing good sleep is essential to helping them avoid a greater risk of using drugs to deal with the stress of insomnia later—and not even that much later—in life. Classically for problems associated with addiction, the ear-lier the habit begins, the longer it tends to persist. Because chemicals mess up sleep patterns, effectively exacerbating the insomnia we're trying to avoid, kids who begin drinking and drugging may be initiating them-selves into decades of erratic sleep, in addition to exposing themselves to the illness of addiction.

All the people in recovery who are discussed in this book—the "expert" athletes and doctors as well as the ordinary folks—offer essentially the same analysis of their sleep patterns. While inside their active addiction, they say, they either passed out or couldn't sleep. And since they got sober and started exercising, eating well, and working on their peace of mind—especially through practicing rigorous honesty and cleaning up their past mistakes (in other words, through taking an inventory and making amends)—their sleep has dramatically improved, if not resolved entirely.

"My sleep was the unconscious slumber of the dead," says Phil, fifty, the foodie we met in the last chapter, who grew up in New York City and has thirteen years in recovery. "I didn't go to sleep. I passed out every night." Phil drank and he was, in his own words, "a major, major pothead. My lungs were shot; my liver was shot. When I got sober, aside from being about thirty pounds overweight, I had a smoker's cough and a green pallor to my skin. I looked like shit, and I felt like shit."

I had trouble believing pot had done this to Phil. But then what do I know? Pot is one drug, believe it or not, that I've never used. I could have copped it in the back of any of my school buses starting in roughly the third grade, but I grew up smoked-out by two parents who each used at least two packs of cigarettes per day, and I've never been able to stand the taste of any smoke in my mouth and throat.

"Can pot make you pass out?" I ask Phil.

"Girl!" he says with some disdain. "That's a pretty naïve one. Pot will knock you out. Pot will make you comatose." A lot of people in our generation or older, he says, were able to use weed for thirty or forty years, but today's pot contains higher levels of tetrahydrocannabinol (THC), the chemical in pot that makes you stoned, so it's much more powerful than the back-of-the-bus pot from my *That '70s Show* childhood.

Because there is so much disagreement about whether pot is really addictive, I ask Phil whether he thought his pot habit qualified him as a drug addict or whether he considers himself solely a recovering alcoholic, and he answers immediately: "Pot is extremely addictive. You put lab rats on steady doses of THC and then stop suddenly, and they get aggressive and kill each other." (He's right: studies of adults in treatment for cannabis dependence have shown that more than two-thirds reported at least four moderate to severe symptoms of withdrawal. The most frequently mentioned symptoms included anger, nervousness, and difficulty sleeping.) Phil also reminds me that THC is fat-soluble, so its metabolites settle in body fat and they take weeks for the body to excrete.

"I was going through a lot of pot," Phil says. "I'd wake and bake all through the day. My first month sober, I was just soaking the sheets every single night. The toxins were just pouring out of me in my sleep."

On the other side of the coin are folks like Joshua, fifty-seven, who has been in recovery for twenty-two years, abstinent from booze and coke. Joshua worked in city restaurants in the 1980s and 1990s, an era when you could find folks snorting lines in practically any urban restaurant bathroom. I ask him whether he ever had insomnia while he was using, thinking of the vivid descriptions of coke- and crack-induced three-day benders in Bill Clegg's memoir *Portrait of an Addict as a Young Man*.

"Did I have *insomnia*?" Joshua says. "Are you kidding? *Yeah*." When he got sober, he says, he spent the first four years of his clean time ("I say four years," he says, but "it might have been two years. I can't be sure. I just was not connected with what was happening") sleeping only about three hours a night. Drinking and coking took its toll on Joshua's body. He had been a competitive swimmer in high school and at Division I Syracuse, but boozing and doing coke stripped the strength off his six-foot frame. "When I went to rehab," he says, "I was 145 pounds." That's a body mass index of about 19—just above where my body was when I started detox.

"I was a daily drinker and user," Joshua says, "and this disease just *took* me. I looked in the mirror at one point and I did not recognize the person looking back at me. My eyes were black."

Joshua has blue eyes. "You mean," I say, "your eyes had dark circles underneath them?"

"No," he says, proceeding to describe not just his physical condition but also his emotional state: "I mean they were haunted. I was gaunt. There was no one there. It was empty. I was skeletal. Looking into my eyes, I felt like I was looking into an abyss."

Like the skinny, haunted, weary woman in the picture described at the beginning of this book.

When I hired a doctor to detox me, it had been years since I'd slept through the night. I couldn't even remember the last stretch of good sleep I'd had, and I'd given up thinking I'd ever get good sleep again in my lifetime.

I was headed toward menopause, and everything I'd read and heard told me that women's sleep slides downhill as hormones diminish. Of course I didn't think—didn't let myself think—my inability to sleep well was the drugs' doing. Drugs *helped* me sleep, I told myself. At the back of my mind I suspected it was because of the drugs' screwing up my circadian rhythms—my body clock—that I was nodding off after I'd put my son to bed at nine, then waking up from midnight until two or three, then falling asleep again until I had to drag my body out of bed at seven. Then, always, struggling not to take a two-hour midafternoon nap.

I should give up caffeine, I would think, but how could I do without my morning cup of tea and my ~~candy~~ protein bar if I couldn't sleep? And by the time I detoxed, I hadn't exercised regularly in years—but this was okay, I ~~rationalized~~ reasoned, because I wasn't overweight. In fact, my skinny ass and legs looked awesome in my über-skinny jeans. And anyway, the only reason anyone ever exercised was to look awesome, right? As for my doctors, they never asked me about my nutrition or my fitness practices. I was, I repeat, Not Overweight, so apparently I was eating well. Also, they didn't get paid to prescribe exercise—they got paid to diagnose illnesses and prescribe medications.

And of course, I never admitted that I wasn't sleeping well, because I was afraid that if I ever confessed I wasn't functioning well in any way, they might decide to take away my painkillers. And how would I "function" without drugs?

When I finally committed to detox and recovery, daily exercise and good food helped get me through the drug taper, and hanging with people who knew how to live sober taught me to begin telling the truth. But when I finally jumped all the way off Suboxone and started living drug-free for the first time in more than a decade, acute and post-acute symptoms of withdrawal such as sneezing, restless legs and arms, and alternate bouts of sweating and shivering jerked me back from the brink of sleep. My body couldn't relax for more than an hour or two at a stretch. The longer I went on struggling to keep up my energy during the day and struggling to sleep at night, the more I suspected life was just going to be a struggle and my body would simply never recover.

If there was one problem I faced during detox that made me want to go back to using drugs—that compelled me, for several weeks, to hide a script for fentanyl in my purse, a piece of dishonesty that provided fuel for a doubt about whether I could live drug-free—it was lack of sleep. *Insomnia is classified as a form of torture by Amnesty International,* I often thought at night when it seemed as if some wicked witch had sneaked in and riveted my eyelids open; insomnia is a "cruel, inhumane and degrading" experience that costs us our memory, physical stability, cognitive capacity. A study published in *The Journal of Neuroscience* in March 2014 showed that, in mice, lost sleep causes irreversible injury to parts of the brain that regulate cognition and alertness. It was the first study to indicate that lost sleep actually kills off brain cells—and scientists now wonder whether the same happens in humans. When our sleep tanks, the rest of life can tank: work performance, relationships, other health conditions. For addicts with chronic pain, this can be a recipe for a relapse. Which is why, when some recovering addicts I knew assured me blithely that "no one ever died from lack of sleep," I decided that anyone who could say this to a newly sober addict had to be a total asshat completely ignorant. I argued with them, and I knew it wasn't my addiction arguing: I couldn't just pretend to be a Navy SEAL about it. I had to protect my sleep or I'd end up going back to drugs.

"That statement—'Lack of sleep never killed anybody'—is not only wrong, it's cruel," says Kevin McCauley, M.D., director of clinical services at New Roads Treatment Centers in Sandy, Utah. McCauley is also a former Marine pilot and Naval flight surgeon, and he's a recovering addict. "Insomnia," he emphasizes, "is *genuine suffering.*"

McCauley, who spent a year as an inmate at Leavenworth penitentiary after his addiction was discovered on the job, advocates for the rights of addicts as patients. He loves treating addicts, he says, and he's the first physician and addictions professional I've ever heard call insomnia "a normal symptom of being newly sober." Everyone else—including, at times, myself—usually treats insomnia in detox and recovery as the elephant in the room, the painful relapse-inducing problem that ought to miraculously disappear if we pretend it doesn't exist and keep marching stoically like Roman legionnaires through our detoxes—and then quite possibly off the cliff of relapse or suicide. Because when people are forced to stay awake long enough, that's what they want to do—they want to kill themselves. Which is what going back into active addiction is: suicide.

"I *expect* to see insomnia in a newly sober patient," McCauley says. "To dismiss the patient's suffering with a snappy and dangerous remark is to invite that patient to relapse. It is the responsibility of the clinician to provide tools that the patient can use to cope with the sleep disorder. And it is the responsibility of the patient to use those tools."

Perhaps there is a reason why clinicians are wont to minimize the importance of sleep in recovery. Although researchers can explain exactly why human beings need adequate exercise and good food, nobody knows for sure why sleep makes us feel better. Scientists have been studying sleep for decades, and they haven't been able to figure out why people who sleep well feel "restored," while people who experience insomnia suffer all sorts of problems, including longer reaction times, impaired ability to perform in cognitive tests, and difficulty learning—in other words, problems negotiating stress. Scientists can't even agree on what "sleeping well" looks like: four hours of deep sleep and two hours of rapid eye movement (REM) sleep? The opposite? Eight hours of total sleep? Six hours? Seven-point-five?

One major problem with studying sleep is that sleeping doesn't seem like it's supported by any evolutionary purpose. For one thing, the need to sleep makes *Homo sapiens* in particular very vulnerable. We're ground dwellers with heavy, big-headed babies whom we need to support for years before they can fend for themselves. We have no easy way of flapping up into the trees or diving into water or holes in the dirt when a predator with big teeth surprises us in our sleep.

But a 2013 study from the University of Rochester Medical Center discovered the first molecular-level evidence that might begin to answer the question of why we need rest, and it supports the importance of good sleep in addiction recovery. It turns out that sleep is the body's neurological housekeeper. Sleep rids the body of toxins. In other words, it's the body's built-in overnight detox process.

Here's how that process works. When we're awake, the spaces between brain cells remain too narrow for much cerebrospinal fluid to flow into the brain. This allows the brain to focus on cognitive functions. But when our bodies go to sleep, those microscopic gaps between brain cells—called interstitial spaces—open up by about 60 percent, allowing cerebrospinal fluid to wash the brain and clear away toxins, otherwise known as "poison." So sleep is one of the body's primary "detoxifiers." David F. Dinges, Ph.D., a sleep researcher and chief of the Division of Sleep and Chronobiology at the University of Pennsylvania, said after the study's publication that this evidence "fits with a long-standing view that *sleep is for recovery"* (emphasis mine).

McCauley admits that, ironically, marching with Roman stoicism and just racking up a few months of sober days will give the body time to start healing its sleep cycles. "If all you do for treatment is handcuff the patient to a radiator and bring them Jack-in-the-Box twice a day for three months, believe it or not, by the end of that 'treatment' you will see some improvements in the patient's addiction," he says. But he says that expecting people recovering from addiction to show so little compassion toward themselves while their bodies are literally sweating and kicking all night will cause untold psychological stress *(stress again!)* that could set back their recovery.

It's tempting to use drugs, either for me or for Jonathan. When it's allergy season and my eyes start to sting, sometimes I take a 12-milligram Benadryl—an over-the-counter antihistamine that's sometimes used as a sleep aid. I stay away from Ambien and other prescription drugs that claim to solve insomnia, not just because they can produce a dependency, but also because they're not as effective as people think. "If you look at clinical trials, they do beat out placebo, but a lot of people don't realize that Ambien adds just half an hour of sleep per night," says Michael Grandner, Ph.D., a member of the Center for Sleep and Circadian Neurobiology at the University of Pennsylvania's Perelman School of Medicine and a spokesman for the American Academy of Sleep Medicine and the Sleep Research Society. Grandner studies the ways sleep is related to various diseases, including mental health and depression, which often factor into addiction.

"There are a lot of things that promote relaxation that don't touch sleep," he says. We can drink chamomile tea, sip Valerian extract (which tastes absolutely disgusting), and they may help our bodies relax, but relaxation and sleep are two different animals, Grandner says. "When you pull all the studies on these substances together, they're no different than placebo for insomnia. A lot of people report they promote relaxation and calm their mind, but for people with insomnia, that's not their problem. With insomnia, there's something blocking your ability to sleep."

Insomnia can make newly detoxed people absolutely desperate for relief. Through my blog, I've received messages from all over the world from people who are trying to detox or who have quit drugs and are begging for help because they find it impossible to settle their bodies down into sleep. As McCauley notes, this is a normal feature of early recovery, and Grandner agrees. "It's a combination of the stimulating properties of withdrawal, coupled with increased stress, potentially some physical pain, and other aspects of mental distress," he says. One solution is to wait it out—handcuff yourself to the radiator. "Acute insomnia typically resolves on its own, given enough time," he says, and some people have found this works for them.

All the doctors I spoke with, when detoxing their patients, avoid sedative-hypnotics such as Ambien and benzodiazepines such as Xanax or Valium. Some readers ask about Seroquel, or quetiapine, an antipsychotic prescribed off-label as a sleep aid. (I mean, an *antipsychotic* as a sleeping pill?) "I don't use Seroquel, because it can be abused," says Steven Scanlan, M.D., medical director of Palm Beach Outpatient Detox, located in the heart of Florida pill-mill country. Scanlan, a board-certified psychiatrist and addictions specialist, detoxed in 2003 from fentanyl using the same method I later used, and he has been in recovery since then. He has helped thousands of people detox from opioids and maintain recovery, and one of his specialties is helping people quit Suboxone. He's one of the only physicians I've interviewed or whose work I've read who can talk cogently about the damage long-term Suboxone use can do to the body and mind.

"For sleep, I use what acts on the histamine and melatonin receptors—the only two receptors they haven't messed up yet," he tells me. And then he tells them to exercise. "Studies show that twelve minutes of exercise per day with a heart rate of greater than one hundred twenty beats per minute restores the natural endorphin system in half the time," Scanlan says. "The people who do that, their sleep architecture returns to normal in half the time that it takes people who don't exercise. *Twelve minutes.* And of course you can exercise more than that."

During my detox, my doctor prescribed me a low dose of trazodone, an antidepressant that causes sedation. I took it a handful of times. For my physical pain, he prescribed gabapentin, a nonaddictive drug used to treat pain, and as a side effect it helped calm my kicking. In active detox, what helped me sleep was moving my body and taking long, hot baths. For me, handcuffing myself to the radiator is not an option. Migraines and fibromyalgia thrive on lack of sleep. So I need to sleep, and I can't take addictive drugs or I'll risk inviting a relapse. I may not like Valium (in fact, I don't like Valium), but Taking Something mind-altering reminds me that there's other stuff out there that I love, and pretty soon I'll be rummaging through people's medicine cabinets. Insomnia is a signal from my body that it needs to exercise more and that I ought to look at what I've been eating. Or else it means I need to take care of my mind. I can do that by asking for help, or by helping someone else. The point of addiction treatment, McCauley says, is not to convince people in recovery to put up with unnecessary suffering; it's to relieve suffering and to teach them skills that will promote healing and bring them back to their bodies. One of those skills is building a supportive community.

One of my favorite addiction recovery professionals and thinkers is the Canadian physician Gabor Maté, who for years oversaw a legal safe-injection facility for people addicted to heroin in the desperate Downtown Eastside quarter of Vancouver, British Columbia. In his beautifully written award-winning memoir of his work, *In the Realm of Hungry Ghosts: Close Encounters with Addiction,* Maté explores what he calls "the generational component" of addiction—a component Maté told me he thinks is missing from the American Society of Addiction Medicine's definition of addiction, which the organization revised in 2011. Any definition of addiction should not "reduce addiction to just a physical disease of the brain," he told me. "It would include the psychological qualities that are present or missing in the addict, including the emotional pain."

Maté sees addiction not as a result of genetic predestination, which he says is impossible, but as one of a number of consequences of adverse childhood experiences. We may carry a predisposition toward addiction in our genes, but it's our environments that determine how those genes are expressed. Kids who don't have the skills to negotiate extreme childhood stress and the community to support them in the use of those skills, Maté says, run a much greater risk of using drugs to numb their fear and anger about the unmanageability of their lives.

Maté's interpretation is grounded in the CDC's enormous long-term Adverse Childhood Experiences (ACE) Study that I mentioned in chapter 1. The study surveyed more than 17,000 people and found that individuals who experienced ordeals such as physical and emotional abuse and neglect, parental incarceration or absence, parental mental illness, and parental substance abuse are much more likely to suffer any number of physical and emotional health problems, including addiction. The more of these traumas the child experiences, the higher the risk. My mother and I both had upwards of six out of ten ACEs. My son had three—two of which, the untreated addiction and depression I had for a while during his childhood, come from me. I know from my research that kids who experience more than a couple of ACEs run a higher risk of all their consequences, including addiction. Of course, I want to reduce my son's load to zero. I don't want him to suffer from my mistakes.

I mentioned to Maté that I've spoken with a number of women in recovery who also come from addictive families and who feel guilt—and, in fact, lose sleep—over their suspicion that they've caused their children to experience active addiction.

"It would be true. The parents' addiction *did* cause the children's addiction—or potentiated it," he said. "That's just a fact. But that fact and the mothers' feelings of guilt are two separate issues. So I would say to any of these mothers, 'You know what, you told me right—your addiction really potentiated your children's. There's no way to get away from that. But you're just a link in a chain: what potentiated *your* addiction?' In other words, you're not a separate person. You're part of a multigenerational family system. And you're part of a culture."

This is part of the reason supportive communities help so much in recovery from addiction. They make up, quite literally, a "counterculture." When I asked Maté—considering the fact that he's such an advocate for harm-reduction—whether he thinks addicts can live drug-free, he said, "The answer is absolutely yes. Precisely because we're not isolated human beings. If you talk to people who have made it, what was the one quality that was always there for them? *Community*. As human beings, we're biologically, neurologically attuned to each other's brains. If I were to adopt an angry expression and say something aggressive to you right now, your physiology would change immediately. We're bound together—they call it 'interpersonal neurobiology.' So recovery very much depends upon the kind of supportive community that's available."

And so does prevention. If addiction is a perpetual motion machine cycling through the generations and steamrollering everything in its path, reversing the cycle of addiction and stopping that steamroller is a gargantuan task. But it's very much a part of my recovery. Because I love my son.

That's an understatement.

When I quit drugs and decided to commit myself to recovery, my son was ten—and insomniac. Two months before I detoxed, my husband and I had sent him with two of his good friends to a four-night soccer camp 120 miles away. I was still using fentanyl when we signed the forms and paid the fee. In my mind piped a quiet voice (which, having for some time practiced rigorous honesty under the guidance of sober people, I now know was my intuition) insisting he wasn't yet ready to go so far for four nights. But I told myself that he was a big boy, he had two good friends going with him, and his father wanted him to go. The drugs paralyzed my ability to honor my intuition and speak from it. So it wasn't until I woke to a collect call placed from my crying son at 1 a.m. the first night of soccer camp that I realized my inner voice had been right: he wasn't ready to go.

Jonathan scraped through that experience, but as summer waned into the school year, his stress mounted, his peace of mind declined, and his ability to sleep fell apart. It was all a bit ironic: I was in detox and also sleeping like shit. So together, he and I confronted our fear of the dark.

Jonathan's fear would descend upon him with the evening shadows descending upon the earth. As winter approached and the sun set earlier and earlier, he would come to me, his brown eyes haunted by fear of his memory of soccer camp—being stuck awake with, as he said, "no one to help me." He'd cling to me almost as if he were three again. "I'm feeling *it*, Mama," he'd say, ashamed of naming his feeling as fear. Because he was supposed to be a big boy.

I found Jonathan a child psychologist, an experienced and sensitive practitioner who might have taught me more than she did my boy. It was on the days I met with her that I realized how thoroughly my addiction had silenced my ability to think for myself, express my feelings, negotiate the stresses of my life. And despite the fact that I'd had innumerable years of therapy, I still thought that loving another person required me to remove all his "negative" feelings and take care of him at my own expense.

After a couple months of therapy, he'd made some progress and could fall asleep on his own. Then my sister brought her three kids for a Thanksgiving visit. For four days the four kids ran around our house like a pack of puppies with Jonathan their alpha dog; then suddenly they were gone and the house was quiet again. And his sleep unraveled. He was back to climbing on me like a little boy, crying every evening at sundown, begging me to cuddle him to sleep—except he was by that time eleven and weighed eighty pounds.

The therapist asked me how I felt about his behavior. Suddenly, I found myself expressing feelings I'd never admitted even to myself: that I was physically exhausted by his neediness, that I was sick of hearing how he wanted a sibling but only a sibling that was the right age and sex and with whom he'd never have to share his space or toys ("You don't want a brother, dude," I told him, "you want a part-time live-in friend"), and that I was frustrated by the fact that he no longer wanted to sleep at his friends' houses.

Instant Step Five, with the therapist.

What a relief to tell the truth. I realized that I'd felt so ashamed of my feelings of frustration, of my resentments about my son's behavior, that I'd kept them secret, even from myself: *Good mothers,* I'd always told myself, *should never allow themselves to be angry at their kids.* I'd suffered enough wrath from my mother that I wanted Jonathan never to feel compelled to take care of me or responsible for making me angry.

But we all sometimes make each other angry. It's just reality.

And because my system of recovery tells me that it's quite literally lethal for me to be selfish, I had decided I'd simply Never Be Selfish Again. Instead, I would Be Recovered. I would Help People. I would be the even-tempered, predictable Jen that I could be when I was on drugs. But it was all a pretense. The numbness I'd felt in active addiction hadn't by a long shot equaled an even temper, and since I had detoxed my body, I was not even-tempered. I was in early recovery: I was volatile, emotional, sentimental, mercurial. Watching the movie *Finding Neverland*, I cried when the kids flew up onto the stage, and I had to admit to myself that Johnny Depp's face got me hot. Reading *The New Yorker*, I would cackle like hell at Roz Chast's cartoons.

On the other hand, a more hopeful way of interpreting this outpouring of feelings is that detox was returning to me the power to feel human emotion. "I start to hear about the positive aspects of the detox as the patient is starting to feel and experience significant emotions again," says Steve Scanlan of Palm Beach Outpatient Detox. "I love hearing the stories from the patients about their rediscovering music and literature and crying easily after meaningful conversations or dramatic movies," Scanlan writes in a paper about his method of detoxing patients from Suboxone. "Medically speaking, I surmise that the mix of intense feelings that are arising signal the beginning of healing of the limbic system in the brain." The midbrain, in other words—the part of the brain that was hijacked by drugs.

In early sobriety I was experiencing my feelings freely, maybe for the first time in my life. And that meant I felt intense frustration when my son would drape his body onto mine at dinnertime and tell me he was freaking out and wanted me to make it all okay. On drugs I had forced myself to believe it was my job to make him okay, but I no longer believed I could do that, and I no longer had drugs to numb my vexation.

As though my frustration had ever been a secret to my son. I realized he had probably always been able to tell I was pissed off—whether I tried to hide it or not. Just as Maté notes that we're neurologically bound to each other, kids have an ultrasensitive radar for feelings. They preternaturally know everything, especially when it comes to their parents' emotional lives. My mother hadn't needed to tell me how angry and frustrated she was; I could see it in her body, in the way she gritted her teeth (a habit all her kids have inherited), in the way she chain-smoked, twining leg around leg and arm around arm, as if to bind her feelings inside her body.

The therapist told me she suspected my son was angry at himself that he couldn't sleep well, and that he was angry at me that I couldn't "fix it" for him. She confirmed my assessment: he was behaving like a toddler again, and he was having difficulty separating from me. In that moment, I realized that I hadn't *allowed* him to separate. I'd been avoiding it. My fear of him moving further away from me, of growing up and leaving me forever—a fear my mother had always had about her kids—was one of the narcissistic fears that drove my addiction. However exasperated I was that he was clinging to me like a little boy, I hadn't let him go, and I myself had set the stage for his unmanageable responses to stress.

"Have you ever read Alice Miller's book?" the therapist asked me.

I convulsively chuckled. When people say "Alice Miller's book" they mean only one of them: *The Drama of the Gifted Child.*

"Why did you laugh?" she asked.

"*The Drama of the Gifted Child*? I read that twenty years ago," I said.

The Drama of the Gifted Child explores the ways in which narcissistic parents damage their kids by sabotaging one of the central acts of parenting, which according to Jung is "mirroring" the child. When a narcissistic mother—a mother who's more invested in reinforcing her own feelings and experiences than in fostering her child's—forces the child to mirror her instead of doing the parental work of mirroring the child, a consequence is that the child learns from time before memory to Take Care Of Mommy at the cost of the child's own needs and feelings. And because kids will learn anything their parents want them to learn in order to survive, the child makes it her purpose in life to keep her mother secure by allowing her mother, essentially, to become a parasite and suck the child's life away. The child does this willingly: she needs security and affection as much as she needs food. So the child becomes very good at doing whatever is required to earn that security.

It's a system that thrives in families in which addiction is rampant.

No wonder. All those midbrain drives for food, self-defense, security, are hijacked by the need to take care of Mommy. Making Mommy Happy becomes the drug. I've seen it again and again in meetings for alcoholic family members. We've learned to Make Mommy Happy. Those of us who have it bad transfer that compulsion onto our friends and family. I learned at a very young age to focus on other people to secure my own peace of mind. Here's proof, from my fourth-grade teacher on my report card:

> Academically, Jenny is doing well but she quite often shows too much interest in other people's problems.

Miller's book was extraordinarily difficult for me to read because it showed me that my mother had not been able to love me. This happened because my mother's parents did not love her, and so on, *ad infinitum* into the generations. As Anne Lamott has written, "Every woman's path is difficult, and many mothers were as equipped to raise children as wire monkey mothers. I say that without judgment: it is, sadly, true. An unhealthy mother's love is withering."

My heartbreak about this knowledge was sealed by my mother's own journals, which I found after she died, in which she denounced my writing as "evil." She called it by that term. Her opinion of me was that I was more interested in drawing attention to myself than in helping anyone else. And even while reading this, I was tempted to believe her, because I'd always believed everything my mother said as though it were the word of God. I had to look at the facts and remind myself that she wrote these words in her journal the very same year I wrote for my newspaper a seven-part enterprise series reporting on a major social problem in the region where I was working. The next year my series won for the newspaper the state press association's top prize—for community service.

It took me a long time even to consider the idea that my mother had been jealous of my education and abilities, chances she'd never had. For decades the little girl who still resides inside me preferred to think I was a Bad Person in order to spare her the label of Unloving Mother. And then I took drugs so I didn't have to care about the nasty truth.

It was about time I grew up.

"I read that book," I told the therapist tersely, "and yeah, my mother used me that way. And I made it my purpose when I decided to have a kid that I would raise him to be more independent. I'd really love him. I'd mirror him, not make him mirror me."

"And you've done a good job," she said kindly, soothing my terseness with her kindness but leaving me marveling, again, that it has always been so goddam important for me to hear those words: *You're doing a good job.*

Then she made a startling observation: "I think you're angry because your son is behaving just the same way your mother used to."

I sat there while this statement reached inside my chest and strummed a very raw nerve in my heart.

"You're saying he's being a *narcissist*?" I asked, in my never-ending quest to keep shit on an intellectual level. Inside, my feelings were about to bust me apart, fizz and dissolve me like the Wicked Witch (*I'm melting, I'm m-e-l-t-i-n-g),* but on the outside I was still way up in my head. Which, it turns out, is one thing my son is awesome at doing: intellectualizing, pushing feelings up into his head. He can think through problems like a champ, and I have rewarded him for this with lots of love—*My Smart Boy!* And what I needed to do, we agreed, was back up, take off some of the pressure I'd placed on him to succeed, and help him stay inside his feelings long enough so that he could know what they were, then say them.

Even if they were three-year-old feelings in an eleven-year-old body.

Because haven't I had three-year-old feelings in a forty-something-year-old body?

So one night shortly after this meeting my husband and I were sitting in bed reading, and eleven-year-old Jonathan came downstairs from the third-floor attic apartment where he keeps his legions of hand-painted Warhammer action figures. I'd joked with him that I would start a game called Peacehammer. He crawled into bed between us and snuggled down and said he liked being with his "peoples." I put down *The New Yorker*; my husband put down his book and picked up *The Mysterious Benedict Society*, which Jonathan had just received for his birthday, and began to read it out loud. I curled up next to Jonathan and put my face against the skin of his neck. I didn't worry about Enabling His Regression or whatever the hell; I didn't do anything, I just lay there, smelling his skin, and my husband finished reading.

Jonathan whined a bit and then quit. I asked him if he wanted to wear my scarf because it smelled like me. He took the scarf and sniffed it and wrapped it around his neck.

"But you're still gonna sit in my chair, right, Mama?"

I told him yes.

"Good, cause for a minute I thought the scarf was *instead* of you sitting in my chair."

"No way, man."

Jonathan kissed his father, then he and I climbed off the bed and walked into his room. He scrambled into his bed and started wrapping the scarf around the boy doll I made him years ago, when I made my nieces stuffed muslin dolls and Jonathan had asked why only girls got to have dolls. His doll is named Frankie. "Frankie likes the scarf," he said, winding it around Frankie's perennially naked torso. It must be said—not just to prove that I am such a frigging awesome mother but also to prove Frankie was not always naked—that I had also made clothes for this doll, jeans and a button-up shirt (with real buttons that work) out of orange fabric that Jonathan picked out himself. But now Frankie looked maybe even sillier wearing my hand-knit fuzzy red scarf wrapped around his body. My son didn't care: he cuddled his doll and I sat in the chair next to his bed and we turned the light out and I put in my earbuds and listened to Sting tell me "Every Little Thing She Does Is Magic" and within five minutes he was asleep.

Some Guidelines

Here are some guidelines to follow as you begin, or continue, to rest in the permanent home that is your mind and body:

- Sleep is the body's natural detoxifier—it fosters recovery.
- Sleep will improve simply by you remaining abstinent, but there are also disciplines you can practice that can foster the improvements. Regular aerobic exercise is an effective way to rebuild the sleep architecture.

- It's tempting to use drugs as sleep aids, but even drugs approved as sleep aids only add thirty minutes of total sleep.

- Sleep is not the same as relaxation. Some behaviors and substances can relax the body, but they may not promote better sleep.

- Practices that foster peace of mind can also improve sleep.

Gratifying the Body
Pleasure and Sexuality

· ·

I lose my respect for the man who can make the mystery
of sex the subject of a coarse jest, yet, when you speak
earnestly and seriously on the subject, is silent.

–Henry David Thoreau, *Journals*

When I figured out that, if I were going to write about physical recovery
from addiction, I'd have to tackle the dodgy subject of pleasure and sexuality, the first person I thought of was Mikey.

I met Mikey on an online forum for people trying to kick opiates.
He was twenty-one, living in the American West, a musician who wrote
songs and had gigged with his band. When he first started telling his
story, he had four days clean off smoking black tar heroin. He was young
enough to be my kid, for godsake, but even so, one weekend Mikey and I
had a long talk about heroin, music, and sex.

There are dirty jokes about sex, and then there is the lighter humor
that comes from trying not to take yourself too damn seriously while
you're busting your ass to overhaul your life, and my talk with Mikey was
punctuated with the latter.

He started off by issuing a Black-Box Warning: what he needed to talk about, he said, contained *(gasp!)* "sexual content." "You may not want to listen since you're a mom," he said. Of course this sweet little caveat only served to tune me in more clearly. *Tell mama all about it, honey.*

Then he began bitching about how many orgasms he was having with his girlfriend.

He complained that he could no longer last "a long time." "While on H, I could go forever and ever—hours at a time" without an orgasm, he said with a bit of nostalgia. I swallowed. *Hours?* "Literally, my girlfriend and I have spent multiple hours having sex and she is amazed with how long I can last," he said. At forty-four—that's how old I was then—hearing these candid admissions from a young man less than half my age made my eyes feel a little hooded and cynical, like Anne Bancroft's in *The Graduate.*

Then Mikey moaned that, whenever he quit smoking heroin and became in the least dopesick, his sexual endurance declined. On the other hand, he seemed to need to have more orgasms. "Now that I'm off opiates, we're going back to the machine-gun approach," he said, "coming quickly but being able to do it again and again and again." (*And again and again?* I thought.)

One of his biggest concerns was the logistics: they were no longer using condoms, he said; using condoms might make her think he was cheating on her, but a condom might help him last longer, and it would make the sheets less messy. "It's no fun having to wash the sheets every time we do it," he said. On the other hand, he said, he didn't actually *want* to wear a condom.

"It's no fun when you can't feel anything," he said.

It was as though using heroin was like wearing an invisible condom, and it was a practice he'd become used to through the years. Heroin numbed out his body's responses enough so that this self-confessed "good-looking guy" with whom "lots of girls flirt" and who had "always been confident in bed until now" could last as long as he wanted to and Look Awesome for his girl.

To make matters more complicated, he was trying to keep his girlfriend from finding out that, in fact, he had a heroin problem. During the times that he lasted a long time without an orgasm, she had begun to suspect that his inability to climax was evidence of a problem with *her* sexuality; maybe she didn't "turn him on" (how I dislike that phrase: as though human beings are switches). Between his confusion about using condoms and his "machine-gun" responses, he was afraid she was going to find out he was a junkie. And of course, the corollary fear was that she would dump him.

While smoking tar, at least he'd known what he was dealing with in his sexuality. He felt as though he could control it. In detox and recovery, his sexual response had become completely unpredictable to himself— and this was creating instability, stress, and a reason to use again. Of course: managing the unmanageable feelings.

"So what do I do?" he asked.

What interested me at least as much as Mikey's questions about his changing sexuality were the fears he was also expressing about his inability to make and enjoy music and stories. As a musician and writing student, Mikey derived enormous pleasure and purpose from composing and performing. While using heroin, he said, his grades always tanked, he never picked up his guitar, and his brain seemed unable to invent good stories. He wound up feeling depressed, deprived, starved for the part of himself that was designed to engage in these activities, and unable to access that part. Drug use shut his mind and body off from something about his personality and consciousness that he described as being "separate from" and "larger than" himself—his creative capacity, a kind of "higher power."

"When I come up with an awesome song or a good story," he said, "it usually comes from a place in me that is separate from the real me."

This made sense to me. I'd noticed years back that when I was taking painkillers, my body and mind didn't want to listen to music. It was as though my ears couldn't pay attention. I'd put my earphones in, click on a playlist I knew I loved, and . . . I heard it, of course, but I couldn't listen. It didn't move me. Then when my prescription would run out and I'd go into any level of withdrawal, I'd find myself listening to music nonstop, with some songs raising the hairs on the back of my neck, others making me laugh or dance or cry. How could that be possible?

There's a difference between "hearing" and "listening." "Hearing" refers simply to the ears' ability to perceive sensory stimulation. "Listening" refers to the complex connection between the body and the mind. To listen is to use the body's perception to make meaning, to be touched and moved emotionally. To care. To feel.

It's no fun when you can't feel anything.

Listening to music is a way to care for myself, and addiction robbed me of it. This experience runs a bit counter to the conventional cultural narrative, which says that drugs actually foster creativity and the best artists need chemical alteration of consciousness to produce good work. "The idea that creative endeavor and mind-altering substances are entwined is one of the great pop-intellectual myths of our time," Stephen King, a recovering alcoholic and addict, wrote in his book *On Writing: A Memoir of the Craft.* "Any claims that the drugs and alcohol are necessary to dull a finer sensibility are just the usual self-serving bullshit. I've heard alcoholic snowplow drivers make the same claim: they drink to still the demons. It doesn't matter if you're James Jones, John Cheever, or a stewbum snoozing in Penn Station; for an addict, the right to the drink or drug of choice must be preserved at all costs."

The cultural narrative is also not supported by science. The initial "buzz" of alcohol, for example, certainly reduces inhibitions, which is to say that it has the potential to call a cease-fire on the War Between the Critics in the artist's mind so that the fingers can more easily do some typing or painting. The buzz may also loosen the reins on any leaps of language or metaphor, what we commonly think of as "inspiration." In my active addiction, I kept a running list of creative people whose work I admired who I thought *needed* to use drugs to be the "inspired" geniuses they were, and many of them were musicians: Janis Joplin, Jimi Hendrix, Gram Parsons, Kurt Cobain, Jean-Michel Basquiat, John Bonham, Keith Moon, Truman Capote, Billie Holiday, Edith Piaf, Frida Kahlo, Jack Kerouac, Dylan Thomas. Hell, Elvis. I mean, some of the work produced by these people saved me in the way preachers talk about being saved. There were nights in my twenties that I might not have come through had I not been able to belt out "Piece of My Heart" with Janis or push "rewind" on Gram Parsons singing "Love Hurts" with Emmylou Harris. It wasn't until after I got sober and they kept dying—Amy Winehouse, Whitney Houston, Michael Jackson, Heath Ledger, Philip Seymour Hoffman, god help me—that I realized that addiction had killed them all. And to hell with "inspiration": Gram Parsons, for one, may not have cut the songs on his best album had it not been for Emmylou Harris's sane work ethic getting the job done.

When we cross the line into getting smashed, nodding out, or tweaking, our brains are less able to make coherent "inspired" leaps. We either get wasted and, frankly, write or paint shit, or we get wasted and sit back and put on Pink Floyd's "The Wall" so we can feel super-chill and inspired. And that's about all we get: a feeling of being super-chill.

Pink Floyd's "Comfortably Numb," by the way? Its working title was "The Doctor." Because that's the super-educated dude—or in my case, the woman—who shoots you up and makes it possible for you to get your ass out there, do your job, "function." *That'll keep you going through the show / Come on, it's time to go.*

Listening to music has, for me, always been almost as important as eating food. Maybe sometimes more important. I was brought up in an intensely musical family. Both my parents played instruments and sang in church choirs. All three of us kids took music lessons from the age of nine, and my sister and I later trained in voice and performed in ensembles. It wasn't as though our family were the "New" von Trapps—we didn't inflict our performances on audiences—but we easily pulled off four- and five-part harmonies that made us happy in our own living room at Christmastime. My primary image of those gigs remains vivid in my memory: my dad, standing tall, his head thrown back, his eyes closed, rocking on his feet.

My father felt the music in his body, and so do I. My mother told me one of my earliest pleasures as a toddler was planting my diapered bottom in front of the "hi-fi" speakers and rocking out to Dad's Ray Charles or Dave Brubeck albums. Later, one of my most prized possessions (and I didn't have many) was a Panasonic AM transistor radio with a socket for an "earplug." The image in my mind's eye of this plastic device, globe-shaped and the size of a grapefruit, advertised as "portable" back then but enormous and cumbersome by today's standards, looks like an anthropological artifact of another civilization, and in fact it was. Back then, there was no instant gratification in the pleasure of listening to music. We had to earn the money to buy whole vinyl LPs. We had to wait for the deejay to play our songs. We had to call in to the radio station (on landlines, through constant busy signals) to make requests. Then, finally, hours later, the deejay would announce, "This goes out to . . . ."

In high school I finally got hold of an FM radio that allowed me to listen to the one actual rock station in town, on which I could hear, for example, Robert Plant sing "Fool in the Rain" and "Stairway." The ability to listen to those voices—Elton John, Jackson Browne, Freddie Mercury, Stevie Wonder, Stevie Nicks—put me in touch with the outside world and with the internal harmony that's a part of my neurology. And it saved my life.

More people than we realize are robbed of these pleasures during active addiction. "I don't even consider music to be recreational since it's so vital to me," says Matthew, the thirty-three-year-old financial analyst and former bodybuilder who used to binge on Ben & Jerry's ice cream. Matthew finds pleasure spending a couple days each month listening to new music and crafting playlists for people like me who like music but don't have time to look for it. I ask whether he was able to enjoy music while he was drinking and drugging, and he laughs. "When I think of the time I was drinking and using," he says, "it was so cold and lonely, and there was no time for music. I didn't practice yoga. I didn't exercise. There was no soundtrack to my life. And there's a soundtrack now." The other day he uploaded into my Google Drive thirty-odd songs I'd never have found without his help. This kind of sharing of pleasures makes our recovery community larger and tighter.

Considering the fact that my teenage kid and I both constantly carry our music in our back pockets, I don't know how I survived high school and college without an MP3 player. Like Mikey, my sixteen-year-old makes his own music—a creative practice that's antithetical to the destructive habits of addiction. To have fun making music, to do it successfully, you have to be able to feel its rhythm in your body. Yet so many creative people turn to drugs to alleviate the insecurity inherent in the creative process. After all, how the hell do we know where the good material comes from? We don't. It moves in and out of us, like breath. Like love. We can't control it.

Maybe one day that movement will stop forever: the ever-present death instinct, even if it's just the death of a part of ourselves, is a frightening prospect that we're tempted to numb out.

"It's not like I consciously come up with the songs on my guitar or the words on the page," Mikey said. "I play my guitar and it seems almost by magic that my fingers find the right chords that fit together perfectly. Or when I write, I just let go and the words flow from my fingers to the page with my mind not interfering at all. Perhaps part of the reason addiction is so common among artists is because we feel like we have no control over our art. It's hard being in this position, because I never know whether one day that magic will stop. But I've discovered that while on heroin my creative ability is deadened."

It's no fun when you can't feel anything.

I had felt the same anxiety when I was just a little older than Mikey. My writing was "automatic," people loved what I produced, I got fan mail when I reported for daily papers, readers clipped my columns. I won awards. I had stalkers. Then I went to grad school so I could work on writing books and found out that real writers (and their editors) call "automatic" writing "a first draft." I loved writing, I even loved revising, and at the same time I was terrified of the pleasure it gave me to play with language and to enjoy the attention my ideas got me when I published them, so I drank. I thought "I" powered my talent. Like Mikey, I never knew whether "one day that the magic would stop."

"Your creativity is not 'magic,'" I told him in my nicest mom voice. "It's a combination of a gift, which is a unique tool nobody can buy, and hard work, which is energy, effort, and love. The discipline of practicing with the tool is up to you, but the tool is yours for life. 'God'/The Universe/ Genetic Selection was planting seeds the day you were conceived and decided, 'Mikey should be Creative. He wouldn't like being an insurance salesman. Let's give him an ear for melody and rhythm and language.'

These traits are part of the fabric of your body and mind. Nobody can take them away from you except yourself."

That's the way it goes in recovery: while I was talking to Mikey, I was also having a conversation with the person in the mirror.

Research has shown since the 1970s that addicts maintained on methadone suffer "endocrinopathy," a fancy term for a hormone system either deficient, knocked off its delicate balance, or both. What's shocking is that clinics have continued to dispense methadone to addicts in opioid-replacement treatment programs with very little, if any, medical inquiry into or oversight of this serious problem. "Opioid-induced endocrinopathy is one of the most common yet least often diagnosed consequences of prolonged opioid therapy," wrote the authors of a 2009 study in the *Journal of the American Osteopathic Association*. Opioids, they wrote, decrease levels of sex hormones, growth hormone, cortisol, and dehydroepiandrosterone (DHEA)—a steroid made, like cortisol, by the adrenal glands, but in greater abundance and as a precursor to sex hormones. Studies show that patients treated with methadone or long-acting oxycodone, morphine, or fentanyl had hormone levels that were one-third the normal amounts. The authors noted that hormone suppression primarily affects people taking daily opioids on a long-term basis—by which they don't mean years, they mean for longer than just one month.

I was more than two years into treatment of migraines and fibromyalgia with hydrocodone and morphine when I mentioned to my doctor that, by the way, I hadn't had a period for a year and a half. My physician was prescribing 150 milligrams of hydrocodone plus 120 milligrams of long-acting morphine per day, and like the doctors mentioned in the article, she never inquired after any irregularities in my menstrual cycle. When she found out I had gone into menopause at thirty-eight—at least fourteen years earlier than the average U.S. woman—she was shocked. She ordered a bone scan, which showed opioid-induced endocrinopathy had caused loss of enough bone density to render me osteopenic: I was well on my way to osteoporosis. I had the bones of a seventy-year-old woman. My physician switched me to fentanyl in hopes it would jump-start my ovaries' ignition. My period returned sporadically, so my doctor put me on estrogen and mentioned the possibility of giving me other drugs to boost my bone mass.

So opioid-induced menopause was another wake-up call: I could not keep taking painkillers for the rest of my life, as my pain specialist suggested I might have to in order to control my pain. If I did, I'd wind up having to take other drugs to counter these kinds of serious side effects.

When I detoxed, I made a commitment to strengthen my body. At first I walked around my neighborhood, mainlining music to keep up my pace. After a couple months of this, I didn't think I was making progress, but I was wrong; my period became regular again, showing that my body was once again producing estrogen. It was healing. Two years into recovery, I returned to tennis, and the next year, with Darlene's help, I completed two rounds of P90X. By the end of those two rounds, I was sleeping well again, and my body's energy had returned. Strength training and any aerobic workout that makes the body pound the pavement improves bone density. Two years into my recovery, a bone scan ordered by my primary care physician showed that I'd gained back most of the bone mass that painkillers had stolen from me—and I'd done it without taking drugs or even a calcium supplement.

"Keep exercising," my physician said, "and you'll be fine."

As chapter 1 notes, opioids aren't the only drugs that mess with our hormones. Many chemicals, including stimulants, alcohol, and other sedatives, interfere with our bodies' ability to produce appropriate amounts of sex hormones, dopamine, cortisol, and other neurochemicals that regulate important functions in our bodies and minds. Inappropriate quantities of these neurotransmitters circulating in our blood put us at risk of anemia, depression, decreased muscle and bone mass, fatigue, inability to balance, weight gain, and a whole bunch of sexual problems, such as decreased libido, menstrual irregularities, and the kinds of erectile and orgasmic difficulties that Mikey was trying to figure out. "I wanted sex maybe once a week—if that," he said. Mikey was twenty-one. For people older than Mikey who have insufficient sex hormones, that frequency drops drastically.

And what happens when we quit drinking and using? If our bodies are otherwise pretty healthy—especially if we support our strength with exercise, good food, and rest—our hormones come raging back. Thus, Mikey's "machine-gun" problem.

The consideration Mikey was giving to his questions about sexuality was important to his recovery. People in recovery from addiction, especially early recovery, are prone to using sexuality to distract themselves from the enormous stresses of early recovery, from paying attention to healing their bodies and minds and solving the problems in relationships raised by their addictions.

"If you're continuing to bombard the pleasure system with intense, undisciplined, not-well-considered acts of pleasure, that system is not going to come back online properly," says Kevin McCauley, M.D., clinical director of New Roads Treatment Centers in Sandy, Utah. While working as a Marine pilot and flight surgeon, McCauley found out how well—at first—opioids controlled the extreme pressures of his job when he was prescribed Percocet for an injury. Repeated exposure to the oxycodone in Percocet, combined with his inability to negotiate his job stress in other ways, led McCauley to start shooting the narcotic pain reliever Dilaudid in secret. Eventually the Marines caught him. His "treatment," he likes to say, comprised a very difficult year serving time at Leavenworth, where the Marine Corps sent him and where he read as much current research as he could get his hands on about addiction. While in Leavenworth, McCauley formulated a clear understanding of the reasons addiction is a disease and not, he says, "proof that we're just dirtbags" and deserve to be locked up.

McCauley lectures widely about "the disease concept," as it's often called in treatment and recovery circles, and he speaks about it in terms of a disordered system of choice and especially pleasure. To understand why addiction is a disease, he says, it's critical to comprehend that re-peated exposure to drugs and unmanaged stress causes a failure of the reward circuit between two parts of the brain: the midbrain and the pre-frontal cortex. The midbrain is a very primitive region that governs the drives involved with immediate survival—the part that McCauley says "we share with animals, the part that gets us through the next fifteen seconds alive." The prefrontal cortex region evolved more recently and its function is to make executive decisions based upon principles, values, and relationships. Addiction, then, can be understood as the collapse of the communication lines between these two parts of the brain. The midbrain, deep inside the brain, sitting at the top of the spine, governs our need to eat, fight, and have sex, and these all make us feel good "because they're all necessary for our survival," McCauley says. "To make sure we do these things, the midbrain makes them pleasurable."

Repeated exposure to addictive drugs bombs out the midbrain, so we no longer care about eating, defending ourselves, or having sex. Instead, drug use moves to the top of the midbrain's priority list. This, he says, is the reason craving—much like the adolescent sex drive—feels like such a life-and-death problem during early recovery, and why, when we give up drugs, we're so tempted to substitute other chemicals and obsessive behaviors. We're not bad people. We're people who need to heal, and healing takes work and time (another one of my higher powers).

"Addiction starts as a disorder of genes and pleasure," McCauley says, "and it ends as a disorder of choice." And he notes that the word "pleasure" is very morally loaded. "It comes with a lot of moral baggage," he emphasizes. "Can you see how a person with a defect in pleasure perception is much more likely to be interpreted as being immoral before they're ever seen as being akin to a deaf or blind person?"

During detox and early recovery, he says, the appetites governed by the midbrain return with a vengeance. We get hungry, angry, lonely, tired—and horny. "When you take out the drugs, the libido comes roaring back. And let's face it, if you can't get laid in treatment, you probably can't get laid," he says.

"It's not that bad, but it's close. It's as if people were like teenagers all over again," says Jennifer, forty, who came into recovery eight years ago, and who was court-ordered back to treatment after a relapse and several DUIs in close succession four years in. "I mean, like, note passing happens," she says. "And then the notes are read to other people. We have to be taught to be mature all over again."

McCauley left Leavenworth for a four-month stint at a treatment center, where he met, as he puts it, "a recovering heroin addict whose libido was coming back too." They were so into the sheer pleasure and apparent freedom of being clean and hooked up, he says, that the minute they saw each other they'd crash headlong into each other's bodies. "At the time, we both wore leather jackets," he says, "and I can still remember the slap of the leather as we slammed into each other."

However, he says, one problem in early recovery is that the frontal cortex hasn't had enough time to rebuild its circuits. Negotiating life's stresses by engaging in obsessive behavior such as binge eating, shopping, gambling, or hookups essentially continues the burnout on the reward circuit and makes it impossible for the brain's executive headquarters to heal and override its pleasure centers. Thus the Twelve Steps' focus on learning to negotiate the stresses triggering fear, anger, and sexual response—the primitive emotions of the midbrain.

"Learning to have sex again is sort of a portal that everybody has to go through as they get sober," McCauley says. When he and his rehab girlfriend started hooking up, he thought to himself, *Wow!—this sex is really great. I can't remember the last time I've had sex like this.* "When the cortex is shut down, but you can still feel pleasure, you've got this unrestrained, undisciplined pleasure," he says. "It's very intense and often repeated, but it's not channeled into anything positive. The kind of sex I was having with this woman was very uninhibited, very honest, but potentially very harmful. It was like what Jerry Stahl wrote in *Permanent Midnight*—he tried to screw his way out of craving." McCauley's therapist warned him that if he continued in this sexually obsessive relationship, he'd have to terminate therapy.

"And I'm like, *Holy shit, what's going on with these people*?" he says. He couldn't imagine quitting the relationship, because it Felt So Good.

"I made the classic mistake," he says. "What I did not realize at the time is, it's really the women who lose out in most of those relationships. Not always—I'm not saying women are victims. And everybody's responsible for their own sobriety, right? But women suffer more from depression and anxiety. They experience a greater danger from the criminal justice system—if they have children, there's this Medea factor where people really hate women who use drugs." And faced with those kinds of stresses, women in recovery look more for emotional comfort, sometimes by confusing sex with love.

Which is, McCauley says, what he was doing as well. "I was mistaking sex with intimacy. My understanding of intimacy is the capacity to be vulnerable in front of another person and to be okay with that. I screwed with her sobriety. I wasn't creating the intimacy I should have been creating with other sober men and using that as a launching pad toward a more healthy intimacy. We were really just using each other to self-soothe or to distract ourselves from our cravings."

McCauley also runs a men-only sober-living house whose staff members, including McCauley, work to teach the residents skills to help them negotiate the daily stresses of life so they can short-circuit the midbrain's cravings and rebuild the cortex's ability to make effective decisions. One of these skills is learning to experience pleasure and seek it out in appropriate ways. "Addiction is a disorder of the brain's hedonic system—its pleasure system. And one of the things that brings that pleasure system back online is a daily, concerted effort to practice normal pleasures," McCauley says. "So that's one of the things we do—every Wednesday night we have dinner together, we talk about recovery, and then we pile into the van and we go bowling, we go golfing—we have fun together. We call it 'hedonic rehabilitation.' Which might sound a little corny, but it's important, and it's a very popular aspect of this program." With the opportunity to develop nonsexualized, trusting relationships with each other, the men have a chance to learn how to create intimacy with other men before attempting it within the more emotionally charged context of sexual relationships.

McCauley thinks the vast majority of all cocaine and methamphetamine addiction in men is driven by the compulsive sexuality fostered by stimulants, a point lyrically illustrated, for example, in *Portrait of an Addict as a Young Man* and *Ninety Days*, Bill Clegg's memoirs about his crack addiction and alcoholism and his subsequent efforts to rediscover and redefine pleasure. "And 99.9 percent of that sex is about one thing: rage," McCauley says. "If you give the male stimulant addict the tools to manage his rage, the other problems improve." Teaching men how to handle their anger works well in a community setting, McCauley says, and for those not in sober-living he recommends a nonsexualized intimate environment such as a men's recovery meeting, where over time men learn that other men can listen to—care about—their most terrifying secrets and still love them.

Clegg, a gay man, found this unconditional love among women—for him, a nonsexualized environment—specifically two women, whom in his book he calls "Annie" and "Polly." Polly, a young woman who earns her living by walking dogs, nicknames Clegg "Crackhead," while Annie, an older woman, affectionately calls him "Lambchop." I ask Clegg, who earns his living as a literary agent working for a massive midtown Manhattan agency, whether he still talks with these women who helped him get sober.

"Every day," he says. "I mean, *every day*. I got an email from Annie today calling me 'Lamby.' These are the people who saved my life."

Eventually Mikey arrived at the conviction that, if he were going to experience any kind of honest sexual pleasure, he was going to have to quit heroin and tell his girlfriend about his addiction. "The more I think about it, the more I believe the best thing to do is to just come clean," he said. "Come clean off drugs, come clean about the truth, and come clean in bed. Pun intended."

Mikey's concerns about his changing sexuality were real and frightening. Here was a young man trying to hold down his scholarship spot in college, his promising creative life, and his relationship with his girlfriend, all the while battling Badass Smack. And he was telling himself he might just have to use again because it would please his girlfriend and make his sex life more "tidy." On top of all that, while looking for help with his problem, he was trying to protect me—a mom—from having to listen to him be honest about his fears. Obviously (like most addicts, like me) he was overly concerned with other people's opinions of him. And maybe he also thought moms don't actually have sex. Maybe he was looking for what McCauley might say Mikey needed: a nonsexualized place to be honest.

"Mikey," I said. "I realize my status as a mom makes it totally uncool for me to be having, or especially enjoying, or thinking about having or enjoying, sex. But let me ask you: do you know that male heroin addicts in detox report spontaneous orgasms? Fact."

A 1972 report on heroin use in Philadelphia debunked a number of myths about people addicted to heroin—including the impression, still more common than you'd believe, that people with addiction have higher rates of sociopathy than people without addiction. It described some of the more common problems we experience in active addiction, among them lack of libido and impaired sexual response. All these sexual difficulties disappeared during detox, and the astonished authors wrote, "There are even reports of spontaneous orgasm in males during withdrawal." (They didn't know about the females, because the sexual response of the female heroin addicts wasn't studied.)

I'd found this article during my active addiction while searching for information about painkiller use and sexual response. What was I doing researching heroin addiction, withdrawal, and orgasm? Well, there you go. It was one of the larger chinks in the dam of my denial about my addiction. I could rationalize the sedate lifestyle (I had chronic pain that made exercising uncomfortable), the lack of appetite for food (I was thin—I looked awesome!), the erratic sleep schedule (we creative types don't live according to clocks), but I had to admit that the drugs numbed out my sexuality—put a rubber on it, so to speak—and that withdrawal made it all come screaming back. In fact, during my addiction I used to throw myself into a little bit of withdrawal, to heighten my response and look amazing for my partner. Also, maybe, to enjoy myself a little bit—but primarily, *to look awesome.*

The manipulation is what made that kind of sex dishonest. I wasn't cheating on him with another person, but I was having more of a relationship with the drugs than I was having with him.

How did I let things descend to this state? I thought. *What should I do?* In this culture it's so hard to talk honestly about sex—or addiction. As I mentioned earlier, I've heard the topic of sex brought up at a recovery meeting only once. It's been a couple years since that "epic" meeting, and I haven't heard the topic repeated. So where are we supposed to look for information if we're confused and scared? We go to the Internet.

After I turned up the article that described spontaneous orgasm in withdrawal, I decided I needed to find out more about my own sexual response. So I bought a vibrator. And that was how I learned that while I was on a steady dose of painkillers nothing in the world could get me off. On the other hand, I discovered that when my body was detoxing, I could have multiple orgasms.

Let me pause for a minute and allow that to sink in.

My first sponsor told me that my Higher Power would use every single mistake I'd made to help other people, if I were willing to have that happen. I totally thought she was bullshitting me, of course, mostly because I didn't think any "higher power" gave a shit about the boring details of my life (I still believe that). Also, I believed that my screw-ups were extraordinarily fucked-up and unforgivable. I still believe this on some level too. But the shame I have about my addiction doesn't hold a candle to the pleasure I feel in sharing with you the following facts:

Fact 1: Female biology makes it possible for women to have more than one orgasm in a row. Physiologically, it's possible for us to have this much pleasure. Psychologically, it's another story, which leads to . . .

Fact 2: Only a small percentage of us allow ourselves to have that kind of pleasure. The rest of us just figure we can't or don't deserve to. Or we don't know how.

I hadn't known any of this before I started drinking in my teens and taking drugs in my twenties. The information is out there. Hell, Lonnie Barbach published her groundbreaking book *For Yourself: The Fulfillment of Female Sexuality* back in 1975, which taught countless "consciousness-raising" groups how to look at their own bodies and give themselves orgasms. I bought the book in the 1980s. But for so many years I felt so guilty about the strength of my sexuality, its inherent allure and delightfulness, so confused about how to handle it, and afraid of what its pleasure meant about my character, that I could not allow myself to own my sexuality. I had to let others own it and then drink or use drugs to numb my conflicted feelings about my sexuality or to manipulate my body to "perform"—to make myself Look Awesome for someone else. Honest sexuality was the unicorn in the forest. It didn't exist.

But it was no fun when I couldn't feel anything.

For me, this is an example of the silver lining of addiction. My addiction and then my recovery taught me things about my body I might never have learned otherwise. I learned that my capacity for sexual pleasure is one of the most amazing gifts of my membership in the female half of *Homo sapiens.* Shame and confusion led me to drug away my erotic responses, and then, inside addiction, to engage in them in manipulative, secretive ways. But once I got sober and I could *still* have multiple orgasms, I decided to stop beating the shit out of myself just because I like sex.

I wish everyone could have the level of acceptance of his or her body that I've been given in my sobriety. I especially wish this for women. For most of my life, I've hated my body. Now I live so much more comfortably inside it that it's almost like I've moved to a different country altogether. That move isn't even complete—I'm not even halfway through exploring that new territory. I can't read a lot of the signs yet, but having crossed the border, I feel so much more alive.

So I told Mikey that women (even moms!) also have lots of orgasms after we detox. "It happens to women too," I said. "Your experience makes me think it's interesting the way the gender roles reverse. Men supposedly get happy when women come at the touch of a button. Women supposedly get happy when men carry on for a long time. If the woman takes 'too long' to come or the man comes 'too soon' or doesn't come at all, everybody's world is rocked. Great rationalization to use, actually, and one I employed all the time."

It's easier to keep things predictable in bed. That way we don't have to risk trying to talk about anything problematic or emotionally charged, anything that might point out vulnerable spots in our armor. God knows, who gets naked and then wants to take the chance of actually being intimate? But that's what recovery asks us to do, and that's one of the ways we find out who we really are, by seeing and touching, and allowing our bodies to be seen and touched. By putting our hands on each other.

"I was thirty-eight years old when I got sober and I don't think I'd ever had an honest relationship in my life," says Phil, fifty-one, the New York City native, who quit his booze and huge pot problem in Seattle. Many programs of recovery advise avoiding new romantic relationships in the first year; Phil decided to spend his first year celibate. "I'm glad I did that, because like everything else that was fucked-up in my life, the way I was using sex was not exactly the healthiest. I think a lot of guys tend to externalize their sexuality. I didn't have much in the way of meaningful relationships. I got laid—for what that's worth."

Phil says that in active addiction he'd used sex as another way to score a high. While getting drunk and stoned, he could just have sex and not care about his human need to be real about his feelings with another person. To be vulnerable.

Vulnerability—bingo. Mikey's fear.

"Think about it," I told Mikey. "You smoke a drug whose purpose-built neurological action is to numb your nerves. For several years, you've *numbed* your nervous system, and that includes the nerves that govern your sexual response. Then you start tapering down. And you expect to be able to carry on with Mr. Slow Trigger?—I don't think so."

About eleven months into sobriety, Phil says, he was in great physical shape and starting to get attention from women, and he made the decision that he was ready to try to be honest in a sexual relationship. "It was springtime in Seattle," he says, "and I was on my Ninth Step. I started dating at that point. Not long after that, I met the woman I ended up marrying." The marriage lasted six years, and although it ended, Phil considers it a successful relationship, because his wife never saw him drunk or high and because he was honest with his feelings.

"You don't get your buttons pressed in sobriety like you get your buttons pressed by a lover," Phil says. "How do you get to practice the principles if you're not allowing yourself to be pressed that way?"

For Arielle, the twenty-four-year-old New York City native who now lives in Seattle, the most important part of experiencing pleasure—whether it be hiking, climbing, cycling, or spending time with her lover—has been establishing a supportive community that helps her accept herself. Before she got sober, Arielle had dated only men. When she moved from New York City to Pittsburgh with six weeks clean, she says, "I was gonna do three things: I was gonna be not smoking, I was gonna be not drinking, and I was also gonna try to be gay." She managed the first two, but the last one didn't work out. As soon as she arrived, she started dating a young man. No surprise, I thought: Arielle is a gorgeous young woman with a sandy-colored pixie haircut and a luminous smile that brings out her deep dimples. Her personality is pure honey, attractive to bees of all persuasions. But in early sobriety, her midbrain stuck to its old grooves, and she picked a dude. "Every time I had sex with this guy, I went to therapy and just cried and cried, 'I don't know what's wrong with me.'" She had dated one girl before she got sober, and she says, "We did not have good sex. It was all tied up in shame and guilt."

Finally she listened to her own body and admitted to herself that she preferred women's bodies next to her skin. "Before I started dating women," she says, "sex was mostly painful, and with a lot of boys, I'd just want to have sex with them right away and get it over with so their penis would not be near my face." This bit of radical honesty, which she says came straight out of the honesty she developed in her relationship with her sponsor and the recovery groups she attended, led her to take the risk of changing her old behavior and start dating women.

"Just having sexual organs that I feel attracted to near my face was a real difference," she says. It reduced her stress and increased her pleasure. Finding support in Seattle's progressive, sex-positive queer and kink communities helped her learn how to talk about sex without shame and guilt and to accept her own desires for pleasure and relationship. "They talk freely about sex," she says, "which I don't think happens in most of society.

"Mostly it was getting sober that helped my sex life," she says. "Sex and masturbation and fantasy life, that's always been important to me. But I hadn't had a community where I could be open and honest. Among my straight friends, sex is joked about. Through sobriety, I really found other people for the first time. I'm so open and honest in recovery and with my sponsor. It was natural to try to find a place where I could be that way with my sexuality."

McCauley sees the sponsor-sponsee relationship and the relationship with one's recovery community—with one's family, essentially—as a collaboration that serves as a "surrogate prefrontal cortex."

"As an alcoholic, I'm prone to paranoia and resentment—the midbrain drives," McCauley says. "My sponsor will act as my prefrontal cortex and tell me, 'Calm down, relax, don't make any big decisions—you're actually a lot happier than you think you are.'"

Collaboration and community in real life (what online communities call "IRL") might have helped Mikey, whose main concerns were having the right number of orgasms at the right time, and not messing up the sheets. I suspected from my own experience that Mikey was focusing so much on the timing and the "mess" to try to distract himself from the real questions, which were whether and how he would be honest with his girl-friend. And underneath that, be honest with himself.

"As for the sheets getting wet," I told him, "fuck that, okay? Do you know how many people would give their right arms to have the kind of sex life that you're having even while tapering off heroin? 'I'm sorry, baby, I just gotta come a couple more times.' Damn. Think about *her* for a minute: Do you know how desirable that kind of honesty can make a woman feel? Do you know how rampant 'sexual dysfunction' is out there—lack of desire, lack of arousal, inability to orgasm? And these are just the psychological disorders. There are lots of physical problems that many people have. Just keep in mind that the orgasmic dysfunction you experienced while using, while sometimes pleasant and dependable, was Not Normal."

The sober people I spoke with who risked talking with me about their sexuality said the best and most pleasurable relationships they've had have been based on shared purpose and mutual help. On selfless-ness, not self-gratification. Matthew, who has been in and out of recovery for eight years and sober this time for four months, is moving through the "portal" McCauley mentions of learning how to have honest sex. He's a former bodybuilder and trainer and a yoga practitioner. His body is so lean and ripped that it may well be the reincarnation of the model for Michelangelo's David—whoever that beautiful young man might have been. Understandably, Matthew says he thinks some women have looked at him and formed certain expectations of him. He learned to make his decisions regarding sexuality based upon not his own desires but on what others expected. Drinking, he says, was a tool to manipulate his decision-making about pleasure, just as McCauley says. "I'd ask my-self," Matthew explained, "'What are the other guys acting like? I can't in good conscience act like that, but I can drink, and once I'm on autopilot I can act like them.' And if I didn't like the expectations women had of me—being a party animal and all that—I could drink and still meet that expectation."

In recovery he has learned he can't have meaningless hookups. This doesn't mean that one-night stands are "unsober" across the board. To the contrary, many people I've spoken with about their evolving sexuality in recovery expressed their growing conviction that "sober sex" refers to sex that's mutually consensual, the terms of which are clear and to which everyone involved freely agrees. Which just sounds like mature sex, right? Yeah, and to manage that, everyone involved has to have a pretty good handle on who they are and what they want—and that's Matthew's point. In recovery he's finding out who he is, and that man can't have casual sexual interactions. "Meaningless romantic encounters don't really happen for me," he says. "Whether I experience guilt or attachment or some kind of ongoing development I didn't plan on—if I go into it thinking it'll be meaningless, there's still more meaning than I expect.

"Flirting with a woman was flirting with danger in some sense, even if it wasn't hurtful in that minute. Or if it affected the friendship, it was like I didn't care. Now," Matthew says, echoing McCauley, "I'm finding that being stronger in my relationships with other guys and people who are my teachers is more helpful than trying to develop my relationships with women.

"I love women," he's quick to qualify. "It's always been really easy to have friendships with women. But if I call someone to hang out, it's a guy. I find that I no longer push relationships with women. I don't push closer to them, and I don't push women out if it seems they're being brought into my life for a reason that's really good."

Mikey eventually told his girlfriend about his addiction. While she went off for a few days to think about what he'd said, his fear got the better of him and he took the bus to the city and copped. But in that time he also got honest with his lead singer and collaborator about his habit. "It feels good having someone that knows. Not a single person used to know I had a problem," he said. "Letting it out takes some of the pain away." He said he wanted to get high from composing, performing, writing, rather than from drugs. He said he wanted to overcome his abusive past, rather than using it as an excuse to get numb. Then he qualified what he meant by "abusive" past: "I got the shit beat out of me every week. I once got my head slammed through a wall, then had to pay for the repair because it was 'my fault.' I once had to sleep on the concrete floor of our unfinished basement for a month because I had gotten in trouble at school."

His frustration with his ungovernable urges spilled over: "I can choose whether to let my past affect me. I don't want to use drugs. It's such a waste of potential. I recognize that, *but I still went and copped. WTF!*"

During the next four years Mikey went out and came back, went out and came back. The last time we heard from him, he'd put together eleven-and-a-half months drug-free. Then, as he said, "I woke up one morning and said, 'Fuck it.'" He copped, used, and overdosed—and fortunately, he lived. I so much admire Mikey: I admire all young people who try to kick drugs. It was impossible for me in my twenties. I didn't have the capacity to try to recover when I was younger because the examples of self-care I'd been given were just too incomplete, too full of holes. I didn't know what the hell I was doing. When I was stressed out, more often than not, like Mikey, I'd just say, "Fuck it." It wasn't until I had my kid and then saw both my parents suffer wretched deaths as a result of addiction that I was able to commit to a system of recovery. I realized that, if I kept it up, I'd be putting my son in the same position I'd been in: looking down at my parents' dead bodies. I told myself I was in recovery for my son. But as I spent time with more and more people IRL, people whose eyes I could look into, people whose voices I could hear, who hugged me when they saw me come through the door and who held my hands when I cried with frustration at my own ungovernable urges—I had to admit that I was doing it for myself. Over time, as I put more and more hours into building a healthy community, learning and writing about addiction, and taking care of and living inside my body, I realized I deserved better than I had long given myself. I learned to love myself. I'm nowhere near where I'd like to be. I'm still a beginner.

The late Sherwin Nuland, a physician and National Book Award–winning author of many works that explored the science of spirituality, saw physical and emotional healing in terms of human beings' constant pull between Eros, which is intimate love, romantic love, in Freudian theory the "life force," and Thanatos, the principle of destruction and instinct toward death. "We are so tempted to go to hell with ourselves, as it were," he said in a recorded interview, "that we actually do come near it, even recognizing the other pole. And this is what the Greeks meant when they were talking about Eros versus Thanatos, the love and life sense against the death sense. I don't think it's in very many of us to deliberately choose destruction, but we play with it and it licks us and burns us and can ruin lives."

That's a pretty good description of craving and active addiction: the temptation to "go to hell with ourselves"—to play with the fire of destruction and, ultimately, death.

But what we're doing in recovery is the tenacious and decent work of getting to know ourselves, of supporting our own growth by turning to ideas, practices, principles, archetypes that are larger and more powerful than ourselves—and more powerful than our illness. The experiences that Phil, Arielle, and Matthew articulated earlier speak to recovery's purpose—deriving pleasure from knowing who we are, what our principles and values are, and making choices according to those.

For the past fifteen years one of the powers greater than myself I've had to admit is at work in the world is the innate urge toward healing designed into our bodies and minds, a birthright over which we have no control through our will. If I cut my finger, I can't will it to heal. The wound won't respond to my simple desire, mental force, or "wish." But I can make a decision to support healing. I can clean and bandage the finger. I can resist the itchy urge to pick the scab. I can get out of the way of the power that was already at work before I cut my finger, and that will continue to work even if I choose to take my will back, get in the way, and frustrate healing. In taking action to support my own healing, I'm practicing the simple principle of self-love, and if the Twelve Steps can be accused of having a "moral" rather than a "scientific" basis, that basis has to be love. The decision to behave morally, with generosity, Nuland said, gives *Homo sapiens,* the animal that has evolved consciousness and spirit, its greatest pleasure of all.

"Given the opportunity to make choices, [humans] will always choose the more—let's use that big word—*salubrious* way, and salubrious in the classical sense of *healthy* way: physically healthy, emotionally healthy, the thing that's going to make it survive and provide it with the most pleasure. And the moral sense provides people with more pleasure than anything," Nuland said. "A sense of oneself as a good person—one whose life isn't sacrificed for others but is based around community and love—gives one a sense of self that is the greatest pleasure that anybody can have."

The decision to make a moral choice often happens for people in recovery inside a critical moment over which, as McCauley might say, our primitive midbrains can easily dominate our prefrontal cortexes. Recovering ourselves, our principles, our bodies in that moment is a process that asks us to pause with ourselves and experience the dangerous feelings of "going to hell with ourselves" inside the moment as it unfolds. And that requires the physical and mindful practice of meditation and awareness.

Some Guidelines

Here are some guidelines to follow as you begin, or continue, to feel pleasure in the permanent home that is your mind and body:

- Addictive drugs affect the central nervous system, which in turn affects sexual response. We can't choose which feelings the drugs numb out.

- Opioid-induced endocrinopathy, or a deficient hormone system, is one of the most common results of long-term (that is, longer than one month) opioid treatment and addiction.

- Addictive drugs target the midbrain (an older part of the brain that governs primitive drives) and disable the prefrontal cortex (a newer brain region that makes decisions according to principles, values, and relationships). Effective systems of recovery calm down the midbrain and rebuild the prefrontal cortex's ability to veto the midbrain's stress response.

- Sexuality does not equal intimacy. Sexuality is a biological response; intimacy is the capacity to be emotionally open and vulnerable with another person.
- Humans' greatest pleasure comes not from sexual response or from drugs but from behaving according to a moral sense.

Awakening the Body
Meditation and Awareness

· ·

This is what you shall do; Love the earth and sun and the animals,
despise riches, give alms to everyone that asks, stand up for the
stupid and crazy, devote your income and labor to others, hate tyrants,
argue not concerning God, have patience and indulgence toward
the people, take off your hat to nothing known or unknown or
to any man or number of men, go freely with powerful uneducated
persons and with the young and with the mothers of families,
read these leaves in the open air every season of every year of your life,
re-examine all you have been told at school or church or in any book,
dismiss whatever insults your own soul, and your very flesh shall
be a great poem and have the richest fluency not only in its words
but in the silent lines of its lips and face and between the lashes
of your eyes and in every motion and joint of your body.

—Walt Whitman, preface to *Leaves of Grass*

Every Sunday when I was very small, my parents would take us to Mass at the Catholic church where my father grew up. It was a church built by working-class Croatian immigrants, and my parents sang in the choir loft. Near the choir loft was a balcony where I'd sit, looking down at the congregation, dotted all over with bubbas in black dresses and long black veils. I was too little to go to Sunday school. I remember being about six and sitting in the balcony with Vi, the woman who liked to look after me while my parents sang. Vi would let me look inside her purse and play with the things I found there—her fragrant pressed-powder compact with the mirror and puff, the brown eyebrow pencil encased in gold, her red lipstick. Vi was an "old maid," people said, but she didn't look like my idea of an old maid. Vi wore makeup and high heels. Vi pinned her hair up in a teased bouffant that was maybe not completely naturally blonde. Vi used to tell my mother how much she liked my wavy brown hair, something that my mother herself didn't often say, at least not within my earshot, which is why I remember hearing Vi say it.

Vi was a hairdresser. For many Sundays she begged my mother for permission to cut my hair, and finally my mother consented and drove us to Vi's house, at the top of a steep brick-paved street in McKeesport, the western Pennsylvania mill town where my father had grown up. My mother, who hated driving our big stick-shift Chevy on hills and in urban places (an aversion that inconveniently crossed the majority of our region's geography off the map), gripped the wheel and cussed at the car's clutch at each stop sign. Once at Vi's house, though, in her little basement salon, the touch of Vi's hands through my hair was soothing in its gentleness.

I liked Vi. Even at six, I understood that she had empathy for a little girl's all-out boredom in church, especially when the priest and much of the congregation spoke Croatian better than they spoke English. (Hell, even when the Mass is said in their native language it's hard for little kids to understand. My sweet five-year-old nephew Kevin, on the day of the funeral of his grandpa, my own father, saved me from desperate grief on the way to the cemetery by piping up from the backseat in a jolly voice his commentary about the service: "That was hardly even in English!") While the priest at the altar and the bubbas in black sang back and forth at each other in heavy Slavic accents, I would slouch out of sight in the corner of the balcony pew next to Vi, examining her wallet, running my fingertips over the red satin lining of her black leather handbag, inhaling the scent of her perfume, her compact, her money.

My mother required us to be absolutely still and silent in church, or we'd get a finger-snap and a glare, which only portended a worse fate after the bells rang. But I had no idea why I had to be quiet, still, "good." So I did what kids naturally do: I came back to my body. I played with what was in front of me, with the Big Girl Toys in Vi's bag.

At some point—I don't know when, because I was too young to understand—Vi no longer came to church. The end pew in the left-hand side of the choir loft had become my spot, and I continued to sit there. I remember asking my mother where Vi had gone, and I don't recall her answer, but I remember the downcast look on her face, and the way she averted her eyes from my question. Years later I was told that Vi had died at about forty from breast cancer, that she had been a single mother of a teenage boy, and that the old ladies in black, jealous of her painted beauty and critical of her preference to remain an "unwed, working mother" had decided to exclude Vi from their society.

But at six, I didn't know any of this. All I knew was that I missed Vi. I missed the way she would pat the spot on the pew next to her and, after I'd climbed up, without my having to ask, hand over her purse for me to inspect and root through with abandon—the purse an unquestionable container of femininity and power. My mother's purse, on the other hand, was one of a few objects in our house, along with the guns, the household ledger, and the booze, that were so untouchable they might as well have had electric force fields around them. I discovered that I missed the place to which Vi and her handbag had taken me in the atmosphere of the church, a space filled with stone statues and stained glass and candles, with incense so strong that it burned the back of my throat.

One day after Vi had gone, I was bored and, completely unconscious of the millennial history of the practice, I stared at a candle. I invented a game: How long could I keep my eyes open without blinking or moving them from the flame? I stared so long that everything around the flame in my frame of vision grew dark, as though the world were a shadow and there was nothing real but that tiny fire, and I could barely hear the priest praying or the choir singing, and I no longer worried about my mother casting her glances toward my seat, or what she might say to me if she caught me doing something bad (or not doing something good). I stared for so long with such a solid stillness that I could no longer feel my legs or my back touching the oak boards of the pew, I could no longer feel my head resting on my neck, and I could no longer feel the pads of my fingertips.

Far from "relaxing" me and putting me to sleep in the pew—another *verboten* act: we were not permitted to sleep in church—staring at the candle had woken me up inside my body. Although I couldn't feel the surfaces of my body, although everything but the flame had dimmed in my eyes, paradoxically I felt more awake and aware than when I tried my hardest to pay attention to the priest.

With my eyes still open, smarting from dryness and blind to everything but the flame, I would wait patiently until I felt a strange tremor in the center of my body, like a guitar string being strummed, like spring sap rising slowly along the stem of a tree. When I could no longer see or hear and instead felt that strange vibration, I knew I was inside the place to which Vi, with her tolerance and unconditional acceptance, had led me: my self.

At age six, I had discovered meditation.

You know meditation is entering its heyday as a U.S. cultural practice when you read in a U.K. newspaper that Google and twenty Silicon Valley CEOs have asked Vietnamese Buddhist master Thich Nhat Hanh to teach them ways that meditation might make their corporations "more efficient." Silicon Valley's incentive to integrate meditation into corporate structure comes from the popular opinion among "lifehackers" that the practice improves productivity at work. But the effects and purposes of the practice are deeper, more selfless, and more transformational than achieving a better bottom line. Rather than making meditation part of the structure, meditation will transform corporations' behavior in society—or so Thich Nhat Hanh himself was reported to have told these business leaders. Meditation is about surrender and change, about easing suffering by breaking craving, about waking up the body by waking up the mind—which is the subject of Willoughby Britton's research at Brown University in Providence, Rhode Island.

"The most powerful way to change your brain is not actually medication—it's behavior," Britton told her packed audience during her 2011 TEDx talk. Britton is an assistant professor of psychiatry and human behavior at Brown University and directs her own clinical and affective neuroscience laboratory, the Britton Lab—which she calls the "epicenter" of Brown's "contemplative studies" community. Brown has been bringing neuroscientists, psychiatrists, and psychologists together with students of contemplative practices, particularly East Asian meditative practices, and as a member of the faculty, Britton studies the neurological effects of meditation on the body.

"Contemplative scientists are people who are trained in the outward technologies like neuroscience—we have training in functional magnetic resonance imaging (fMRI) and electroencephalogram (EEG) and all that," Britton says. "But we're also trained in the inward technologies, which came from contemplative traditions. I see contemplative studies as the application of the basic neuroscientific principle of experience-dependent neuroplasticity."

Huh?

"That's a complicated way of saying, *We get good at what we practice*."

I originally talked to Britton to get her thoughts on ways meditative practice might help people in recovery sleep better. She bristled slightly at my questions, and after I read a literature review she published in 2014 in the *Annals of the New York Academy of Sciences*, I could see why. Entitled "Awakening Is Not a Metaphor," her paper is a lucid explanation of the ways in which Western medicine and psychology have fostered a persistent misconception that meditation and "mindfulness" are essentially relaxation exercises that can be used to promote better sleep—and how scientific evidence shows these practices, to the contrary, quite literally wake us up. Britton says she is the only neuroscientist so far who has measured brain activity during sleep in people practicing mindfulness. In one study, her subjects reported they slept better, but the scans showed they actually awakened more frequently and their brain activity showed they were sleeping more lightly—which, Britton says, doesn't necessarily mean they got worse sleep.

"I've been working very hard to counteract this very, very pervasive idea that meditation makes you sleepy," Britton tells me.

What she is discovering about the effects of meditative practice on the brain picks up right where Dr. Kevin McCauley left off. McCauley noted that addiction hijacks the limbic system, short-circuiting communications between the primitive midbrain and the prefrontal cortex, the newer part of the brain that makes decisions based upon values, relationships, and principles. Britton has found that meditative practice restores to the prefrontal cortex—or "the PFC," as she calls it—its superhero powers. It gives Thor back his hammer; it sticks the arc reactor back into Iron Man's chest. It is a source of Power. Meditative practice rips the PFC's six-pack and puts it back into form for making wise executive decisions. And this kind of practice is not sleep-inducing. It doesn't jazz you like a cup of java or a line of coke, either.

It simply wakes you up. It puts mind and body back together.

Britton tells me a story: "I used to play ice hockey, and we could only get rink time at eleven at night. I'd get home at one in the morning and I'd want to lift weights—I was so amped. I'm a runner, and I've been running a couple hours a day, and I sleep like a rock 'cause I'm so tired. But the hour or two after I run, my body can't relax. It's a very similar kind of thing with meditation. If you meditate, you're taking down your limbic system"—your midbrain. "You're gonna be awake—you're gonna be exerting control over your limbic system"—with your prefrontal cortex.

Meditation is push-ups for the executive brain. It creates new, positive "neural networks" that counter the damaged ones created by addiction's bad habits. "In all the cases of psychological disorder where there's negative emotions—in depression, anxiety, obsessive-compulsive disorder, addiction—people have a hard time controlling themselves. The one brain situation common among them is that they have a weak prefrontal cortex," Britton says. And there are many different ways to practice meditation and mindfulness, "so it's a bit messy," she says, "but in general one of the most common effects is [that] you're gonna be regulating your attention. If you do that in a disciplined way, like exercise, it's reasonable to expect that the areas of your prefrontal cortex that make executive decisions will get bigger. Rehabilitation of the prefrontal cortex is the name of the game."

In her TEDx talk, she demonstrates the power of practice by asking listeners to close their eyes and think of something they dislike about themselves. I immediately think: my belly, my judgments, my fear of failure. She tells listeners to open their eyes, asks those who cannot think of anything self-critical to raise their hands, and of one hundred twenty in the audience, she counts only three.

"Okay, so that's a very strong neural network you got going there," she says. "You're basically Olympic athletes of self-criticism. So you've been practicing that habit for a very long time, probably every day—and probably every hour, and maybe even moment to moment. And I chose that particular neural network and mental habit because that is one of the foundational ones that, when it gets really big, it becomes major depression."

Her scientific inquiry focuses on whether individuals are aware, or *mindful,* that they're practicing destructive mental habits, and if so, whether they actually want to be practicing them. "If the answer is no, then I wonder what other neural networks you're strengthening unintentionally," she says.

She then asks the audience to think of the people who exerted positive influences on their childhoods, and to name the qualities of character they admire in those individuals. Audience members volunteered qualities such as humor, strength, perseverance, caring, energy, patience, kindness. "I want you to look inside yourself to see how much of those qualities you have," she says, and I think to myself, *She's basically asking me to look at my shortcomings and assets—Steps Four through Seven.* "Based on what we know from contemplative neuroscience and what we know about neuroplasticity," she says, "we can actually start to think of these things—kindness, energy, compassion, generosity—not as innate qualities that you have or don't have, but as skills that you can cultivate through practice and training." So we can discern which behaviors are productive and which we want to change, and amend the latter (Step Ten).

"And we know from the neuroscience that these practices actually do cultivate these qualities," she continues. "We also know that the neural networks that subserve these qualities can be modified through training."

So we can heal our brains from all sorts of disorders, including addiction, through training our attention. Through, essentially, taking Step Eleven.

It's interesting to think about the number of people who are basically following the Twelve Steps in their lives without even knowing it.

Using meditation to help heal addiction is what Judson Brewer is doing at his lab. Brewer is a psychiatrist at the Yale School of Medicine who trained in mindfulness meditation while a medical student at Washington University in St. Louis, Missouri. During the past thirty years, an increasing number of medical professionals have studied mindfulness-based stress reduction (MBSR), the protocol pioneered and extensively tested by Jon Kabat-Zinn, founding executive director of the Center for Mindfulness in Medicine, Health Care, and Society at the University of Massachusetts Medical School.

As a medical student, Brewer had been studying the effects of stress in mice, but after learning to practice meditation, he evidently decided it might be more useful to study stress in his own species. So he switched his research focus to the connections in *Homo sapiens* among stress, mindfulness, and "the addictive process," as he calls it.

Brewer's Yale lab researchers are finding that mindfulness (in other words, meditation, Step Eleven) is twice as effective as leading medical treatments (read that as drugs, including nicotine vapor devices, patches, gum, and Chantix) developed for smoking cessation. His studies show that meditation tones down the domination of craving (midbrain) over the decision to smoke or not to smoke (prefrontal cortex). The smokers he trains in meditation are twice as likely to break the compulsion to smoke, with no pharmaceutical cessation aids and fewer cravings. Mindfulness training, he wrote, "may help individuals 'sit with' negative affect, cravings, and nicotine withdrawal without habitually reacting to these unpleasant states by smoking." He went on to say that one unique quality of mindfulness training with respect to recovery is that it builds an ability to distance ourselves from intense and dangerous feelings. "In doing so," he wrote, "individuals may learn to (literally) not take affective and withdrawal states personally, which may help them quit smoking."

I know you're already thinking *If it works for nicotine, surely it'll work for booze/dope/coke/meth/Xanax.* I thank my lucky stars that I've never smoked, but I can't tell you how many garbage-can junkies have told me that they had a tougher time putting down their Camels for good than they did kicking any "hard stuff."

The mind makes the decision to smoke; the body actually buys the cigarettes, flicks the Bic lighter, touches flame to tobacco. Inhales and exhales. Sighs as the drug hits. The anticipation of all these acts—as Britton might say, the well-worn "neural networks" created from all that practice—leads to craving inside the mind that is felt by the body as a need: the drug moving to the top of the midbrain's list of priorities.

"It's like he's inhaling the last thing on earth that's gonna give him any relief," Heather, the former heroin addict who now works at Chapters Capistrano, says of her boyfriend's craving for cigarettes. Heather recently quit, an intention made much more difficult while she's living with a partner who's still smoking. As I write this, Heather has more than one hundred days free from nicotine. She doesn't really meditate, she says, "I'm a bad meditator. I'm also a bad pray-er. I talk with my sponsor about this all the time—it just doesn't come naturally to me." Does it "come naturally" to anyone? I chanced upon it when I was six only because I was stuck in church with a bunch of black-veiled bubbas and nothing else to do.

But the practice of meditation, as Britton and Brewer are exploring it in their labs, might be the doorway between the mind and body. The researchers who study it and the people who practice it say it is the mind's gym, it puts Teflon coating on the mind's sticky obsessions and compulsions, and it trains us to let go of thoughts onto which the mind naturally clings, especially habitual negative judgments that may not be true but that we practice over and over anyway. Britton used the example of the string of self-critical monologue; Brewer uses the example of Lolo Jones, an Olympic hurdler who tripped when it looked like she was set to win gold in the 100-meter hurdles in 2008 in Beijing, China. Jones "over-tried," he says—she tried too hard to do well. She let those habitual self-criticisms creep in, she doubted her capabilities just for a split second, he says, and that doubt caused her to trip.

Another way of saying it is that she craved that success, and the opposite side of the coin of the craving is the judgment, the fear of loss. The desperation, the stumble, the actual loss.

With mindfulness, Brewer suggests, she could have neutralized her mind's self-judgments and freed her body to do what she had trained it to do, thereby increasing her chances of gaining her goal. His former smokers use the same principle. In their meditative practice, they train in letting go of the craving, in experiencing the truth of that well-known recovery adage that drove me absolutely batshit when I first quit drugs: "This too shall pass."

I was maybe a week clean and bitching to my online sober pals about how tired I was and how lousy I felt when one of my new forum friends suggested I meditate. Janice, a former high-fashion model and heroin addict, now a softball-playing Jersey shore mom—a woman with long-term recovery whose calm online voice pierced through my sick self-pity and craving for approval—encouraged me to sit for two minutes per day. *God almighty,* I thought, *what the hell is two minutes a day going to do for me?* I was used to Taking Something that packed a quick, powerful load against my fear and loathing and physical fatigue. Two minutes sounded pitiful and frankly useless. But I was tempted: Janice herself was spending part of her Saturdays sitting at a zendo, a Zen meditation center, for more than an hour. Because I wanted what Janice had (I still, in fact, want what Janice has), I tried what she suggested.

I have tried a lot of meditation methods and gear during the past twenty-odd years. I've tried cushions, benches, and chairs. I've tried sitting cross-legged, kneeling, lying down, and walking. They all have some commonalities, I now realize. Janice gave me simple instructions. "I meditate every morning, as soon as my son gets on the bus for school," she wrote. "I bought a meditation cushion, and I sit. I stare at the wall, eyes half open. My sponsor had me begin at two minutes in the morning and two minutes at night, on a timer. Two minutes seemed like two hours. My mind raced, I was uncomfortable, but I did it. In doing, we succeed." We get good at what we practice.

I did what Janice told me to do. I had sat in meditation before, but doing it chemical-free made me understand in an entirely new way how much the act of sitting in meditation is a *physical* practice. We may think of meditation as a mental exercise that happens inside our skulls, but it requires me to sit my body still. I have to pay attention to the breath that moves in and out of my lungs, apparently beyond my will: I can try to exert my will over my lungs, I can hold my breath until I'm blue in the face, but I can't suffocate myself. I'll pass out, my body will save me, that's how powerful *Homo sapiens'* urge is toward healing and life.

My back hurt, my shoulders hurt, I felt dumb just sitting there, I couldn't stop my thoughts. I also felt fat: my breath made my belly bloom outward and, despite the fact that I was alone, the fear rose that someone would see me and think I was fat. Unbelievable vanity. My mind ran around like a rat in a stairwell. I wanted to check the timer. I decided I was a failure because I couldn't stop my mind from thinking.

A lot of people feel this way when they practice meditation. Or when they think about practicing meditation.

"I think a lot about meditating," Arielle, the Seattle cyclist and mountain climber, says. "I have this app, so maybe I do it for a week and then I don't do it for a month. My sponsor does it for thirty minutes a day, but I feel like I don't have enough time to sit still for five minutes!" She laughs at the irony. "I also feel, when I'm in meditation, like I'm a failure when I'm thinking of other things, which is probably 99 percent of the time. I don't like not feeling good at something that seems like it should be easy."

Because I had told Janice I would try, I kept trying. Practicing according to Janice's instructions, after a few days I was surprised: I could feel my mind letting certain thoughts just slip away without panicking. It was as though a fine layer of Teflon coating had been sprayed onto the surfaces of my mind. Eventually, during meditation, I began to feel as though I were sitting in a kayak on a calm pond, with all my thoughts written on the surface of the water, and I watched as they passed by my boat, untouched. I was tempted to reach out and touch them, but I chose to keep my hands inside the boat, on my thighs, where Janice had told me to put them. The physical relief I felt just by practicing this mental discipline was unprecedented—even compared to the effects of drug use.

Because when I was using drugs, they always ran out. But this practice was a renewable resource. I could choose what to think, and thereby choose what my body would do—and what it would not do.

Just like exercise, nutrition, and sleep, though, meditation has been an on-and-off practice for me. When I practice it, I get better at it. When I stop, the muscle weakens. But practice built on good early instruction develops muscle memory and healing, what Britton would call "neural networks" and "neuroplasticity." So as with tennis, the more I practice, the easier it is to pick up again after I've put it down.

According to a comprehensive literature review published in the *Harvard Review of Psychiatry* in 2009—before Judson Brewer's work with smokers—not much scientific evidence exists to underpin the power of meditation to help recovering addicts stay away from drugs and addictive behavior, but this is because not many randomized controlled studies have been conducted on the various modes of meditation. It's also because "meditation" consists of so many different practices that are mixed with so many other different disciplines and therapies. "Despite the paucity of evidence," the authors wrote, "the theoretical basis for meditation's role in addressing substance use disorders is compelling." People with addiction have problems regulating their impulses, the authors wrote, and meditation might be able to help people recover from addiction in these ways:

- increasing blood flow to the parts of the brain associated with executive functions—the prefrontal cortex—and fostering their "neuroplasticity," or those regions' ability to heal and grow stronger

- calming the fight-or-flight response and raising into dominance the rest-and-digest or feed-and-breed part of the nervous system

- "reorganizing" regions of the brain to become less emotionally reactive and promoting healthy decision-making in response to the "triggers" of addiction

- reducing stress-hormone levels, lowering the potential for craving and relapse in response to stress

- strengthening the practitioner's ability to respond to events and to themselves less critically, lessening the craving for a drug to manage damaging self-critical thinking

And though it can't be measured or studied, the authors noted, it's important not to ignore the potency of the kinds of "spiritual awakening" the Twelve Steps mention. "Higher measured scores of . . . spirituality have been associated with better health in many domains among drug users," they wrote. "[A] transcendent sense of self, a metaphysical framework that provides meaning and coherence to one's life, and spiritually mediated self-efficacy have all been suggested as possible factors" in the healing that systems of spiritual growth give to people recovering from addiction.

Of course, if I'm going to talk about meditation with regard to recovery and the Eleventh Step and "systems of spiritual growth," I also have to talk about prayer, which means I must confess that I have no idea how to talk about prayer. Maybe the only way I can broach the subject is just to say what I do, and that's so simple that it's going to sound pretty stupid. The first thing in the morning, when I open my eyes, hardly before I even move my body, I say to myself, *God help me*. It's basically a kick in the ass to punt me over the first hurdle of the day, which is just getting out of bed. Because usually when I wake up and open my eyes, I find my mind is already halfway through laying the bricks in whatever wall I'm building that day—the one that's going to protect me from the shit that my mind automatically predicts is going to fly. It's just the way I grew up. The shit flew, and I learned to build walls to protect myself—control the uncontrollable.

God help me.

Anne Lamott is someone I sort of consider to be one of my long-distance twin big sisters in both recovery and writing. The other is Mary Karr, who swears a lot (which, for obvious reasons, I appreciate) and who once told the *Paris Review* she asks "God" to tell her what to write. Both of them were stone drug users and are now abstinent, and they are able to be utterly themselves in their prose, which I admire. Anne Lamott would tell me "God help me" is an awesome prayer, because it's the first of her

Big Three: "Help, Thanks, Wow." But here's where I get into trouble: If I say "God help me," who is "God"? Which may be why Annie stripped it down to one word: "Help." However, Annie (like a lot of her readers, I imagine, I call her "Annie") in fact believes in "God," and so does Mary Karr, and so do a lot of other people. Maybe you do too—and if you do, I'm totally happy for you, and I would like to know how you do it. Because I don't believe in "God," and I sometimes think it's a hell of a lot easier to face the whole "higher power" thing in recovery if you do. I can't. At least, I can't believe there's a guy in the sky who has plans for the members of *Homo sapiens*. (If there is, it seems to me that we're screwing up a lot of those plans, which I do not think would include genocide, white phosphorus, oil spills, land mines, and factory farming.)

But if you've read this far, you'll see that there are other powers I "believe" in: Light, which shows the truth and ensures that more will always be revealed. Darkness, which, if I resist using it to hide, teaches me about the parts of myself that need care and attention. Gravity, which teaches me humility (what goes up, dammit, must come down). Time, which doesn't heal all wounds, but which heals many of them. Love, the only one of these that's not a property of physics. That is both a feeling and an action. That is a mystery and is most powerful and transformational.

By saying I "believe" in these powers, I mean that I try to go along with them, rather than fighting them. So I guess that's what praying means to me: aligning myself with these forces.

For a long time on my blog I've been calling for Nora Volkow, director of the National Institute on Drug Abuse, to scan my brain or the brains of other people with clean-and-sober time to give us an idea, not of what our brains look like on drugs, but of what they look like on recovery. This is an important question. We're given all kinds of pictures of illness; it's easy for us to imagine illness and then, because the images are so clear, to descend into worst-case scenarios. But when are the scientists going to help us see what it really looks like to be healthy? There's not much financial incentive for researchers to study solutions that can't be patented. But there's a guy who is answering my "prayer." Marc Galanter, M.D., professor of psychiatry at New York University and founding director of its division of alcoholism and drug abuse, as well as senior editor of the journal

Substance Abuse, is sticking people with long-term recovery from addiction into fMRI scanners and studying the effects of AA's and NA's classic prayers on their brains. He's essentially shooting live-action neurological video of the "spiritual awakening" that recovery promises.

"I thought one discrete and explicit way one might do that is to present triggering images to people after they've recited AA prayers and after reading neutral material, and see if you get different imaging responses," Galanter says. By "AA prayers" Galanter is referring to, for example, the Third Step prayer and the Serenity Prayer, both of which essentially orient the mind toward surrender and acceptance of the uncontrollable. Galanter's study is still in progress, but his initial data harmonize with McCauley's and Willoughby's ideas about the ways craving and meditation work.

"We get a very interesting response. The correlates of craving are diminished after prayer," Galanter says. Cravings show up in the midbrain, he says, and attempts to suppress or control craving show up in the prefrontal cortex. And Galanter's team is finding that when people with long-term recovery who say they've had a spiritual awakening put themselves in touch with that power, whatever they conceive of it to be, it calms down their midbrain.

"It's becoming apparent that there's some physical transformation people undergo when they have a spiritual awakening that changes the processes of addiction in their brains," he says. And Galanter said the results are not related to how often people go to church or whether they identify themselves as religious. They're related to people's idea of surrendering control of the uncontrollable to a power that is not themselves.

He has presented these preliminary findings at grand rounds at NYU and will present them in the coming months at other teaching hospitals.

Just as corporate managers and scientists use certain language to describe the effects of meditation, meditation practitioners themselves have particular language for the ways meditation acts upon the body, on the mind, and eventually on society. Shambhala Buddhist practitioners, for example, speak about meditation uncovering humans' basic goodness—

the "brilliant sanity" that they say is the bedrock of human character, which becomes obscured by the kudzu and detritus of judgment and narrative, the "storylines" our egos compulsively craft around many of our feelings.

"Our addiction itself starts with wisdom and sanity. Gluttony, for example, starts with a flash of appreciation, which gets covered up with the panic that *I'm poor; I'm not gonna get enough.* But the ground is wisdom—that appreciation," says Scott Perkins, development director for a Washington, D.C.–based nonprofit and a teacher of Shambhala meditation. Perkins came to Pittsburgh to facilitate a full-day "Heart of Recovery" Buddhist meditation retreat for people recovering from addiction. He has been sober since Christmas Day of 2005. That Christmas Eve, he drank himself into blackout, for which his husband, Jonathan, wound up having to call an ambulance to rush him to the emergency department, where a doctor bored the last hole through the wall of denial the two men had spent years building around Perkins's alcoholism.

"The ER doctor said, 'How much has he had to drink?' And Jonathan said, 'We had a Bloody Mary at two o'clock,'" Perkins tells me. "She said, 'No. He has a blood-alcohol level of point-four—and he's sitting on the gurney answering questions. This is what we call a professional.'"

Perkins was referred to an intensive outpatient program at Washington, D.C.'s Kolmac Clinic, whose staff he says saved his life. They put him on daily doses of the alcohol antagonist medication Antabuse, educated him about the physiology of addiction, and introduced him to recovery meetings. After he was sober for a year or so, he says, he realized he missed the intensive recovery community of his outpatient program, so he started a weekly "Heart of Recovery" meditation session at the Shambhala Center in Washington, D.C., where he had been studying and teaching Buddhism for more than ten years. Shambhala is a strain of Buddhism founded by Chogyam Trungpa Rinpoche, a prolific Tibetan writer and teacher who also happened to be a notorious drunk.

I look at Perkins and realize Shambhala Buddhism has been wandering across my radar for years. My own sponsor is a student of Shambhala. A fellow blogger introduced me to Susan Piver, an author and Shambhala teacher whose twice-weekly free online meditation videos, called "The Open Heart Project," have helped me stay on my game. Even the little

Pittsburgh Shambhala Center has a weekly "Heart of Recovery" meeting, at which we meditate for half an hour and then talk about recovery and meditation. My online friend Janice sat zazen, a Japanese practice, but because I wanted what Janice had—peace of mind and clarity—I knew I would have to meditate with a bunch of other people the way Janice did each week, and the Shambhala Center seemed to be a good place to start. At first I carried a bit of a chip on my shoulder about Shambhala's founder. What sense did it make to practice a discipline created by a drunk? Once again, music helped me. One day, as I listened to Lyle Lovett sing one of my favorite Townes van Zandt songs, I realized, *Am I gonna stop listening to Lyle sing Townes just because Townes was a stone addict who died of his disease?*

Scott Perkins, who started drinking before he was old enough to drive in his native rural Michigan—where there was nothing to do, he says, but learn to skip stones on gravel roads and, of course, drink—says practicing meditation for years before he got sober gradually drilled holes through the denial that drove him to hide his addiction from his partner and even from his own conscious awareness. "Regular meditation practice perforates the solidity of our false conceptions—this cloth, this cocoon that we weave around ourselves for protection," he says. "If you perforate it enough, the denial eventually starts to fall apart." But it takes practice. "I'd spent years spinning this cocoon that would insulate me from the reality of my own drinking enough so I could continue it—such that I could keep my husband from knowing how much I was drinking. Without my meditation practice, though, I would still be drunk and probably dead."

Perkins notes something that I've noticed about my own drinking and drug-use history: the fact that, even in the midst of harebrained, even criminal behavior, I experienced moments in which I knew I needed help, that I was going to have to find a way to stop or else face jail time or maybe death. This is an example of humans' "brilliant sanity," he says. Truth and health can coexist alongside deceit and destruction.

"I remember the numerous times this basic goodness, this sanity, shone through," Perkins says. "The ground of our being is this brilliance. No matter how painful our habitual patterns are, whenever there are gaps, it shines through. There would be a point in my commute to work that the thought arose *Maybe you shouldn't drink*. That's sanity, in the midst of the worst part of my addiction." So despite what we might be told when we first come into recovery, *not* everything that we do before we get sober is wasted.

As someone who has seen people I love die of the disease of addiction, I've often wondered how I managed to survive. The answer remains a mystery to me, but if a reason exists, it might have to do with my ability, at age six, to stare into a candle's flame and feel the life inside my body. I've found myself writing about this life force in various ways since I was an undergraduate studying D. H. Lawrence's novels of class and sexual conflict, and for many years, one of my higher powers or healing powers has been that life force, the inward urge toward well-being built into the body and mind. While working on this book, I had a conversation with Don Miguel Ruiz, author of *The Four Agreements,* about the body's power to heal—and how this power sometimes fails because of the body's frailty and limited material resources. "I watched your talk with Oprah," I tell him, "and she asked you where you felt most at home. And you said, 'In my body.'"

"Yes," he says, looking into my face with an easy smile.

"But what about those of us who feel not at home in our bodies?" I ask. We find them either too large or too small, too weak, too sick, too unattractive, too uncomfortable—and we want to numb our self-criticism.

"These people don't have awareness," he says. "They really feel that they *are* the body."

So in other words, mind and body are not just connected, they are one and the same thing—but they're *not* one?

"The body is matter," says Don Miguel, who is a physician. "You remember physics: matter can only be moved if a force moves it. Matter by itself cannot move. And your body is matter. So then, who's moving your matter?"

I think for a moment. "I don't know," I say.

"That force," he says. "That force that is moving your matter—that force, I call it Life."

The life force. The stream of life. Scientists and writers and artists have created works about this for centuries, because it's so powerful, determined, mysterious. I can practice hatred toward myself and I can hold my breath, but I can't suffocate myself, because my body and mind are designed to protect my life.

So *life* is now one of my higher powers. I align myself with the direction toward which life seems to be pointing.

But what about people whose bodies are sick, who feel as though their bodies have betrayed them? Medical science has given us so many ways of keeping the body alive despite its collisions, its breakdowns, its engine-block lockups.

Miguel (he had greeted me with an enormous hug and asked me to call him "Miguel") compares the body's matter to a machine—a car, for example. "It's like you have the car, the motor starts failing, you can do whatever you like as the driver, but the motor is still failing."

The metaphor doesn't quite play out, of course, because the mechanic can replace parts and do bodywork and keep a car running forever. But the human body suffers inevitable breakdown. So the body is finite, it won't last forever, and we just have to know this. We have to accept—despite the lure of medical technology that would have us believe we may never have to die—that it's going to break down and quit. So it's not a betrayal, it's just reality?

"It's the truth," he says mildly.

This strikes me as so simple and clear as to be laughable. In fact, I laugh. Our society comes up with all kinds of names for "truth": "reality," "actuality," "clarity." "Authenticity" is a big one right now, along with "vulnerability" and "wholeheartedness," we hear all the time that "wholeheartedness counters shame," and I'm down with these terms. I'm all for them. I love the work of Brené Brown, whose viral TED talk and popular books have made them ubiquitous. But why not just use the simplest term?

Truth. That's now another one of my higher powers.

The truth is what kept drilling through the wall for Perkins: he would have to quit drinking, clearly, or else he would die. It was his inexorable, if fragmented and sporadic, attention to the simple brilliance of truth that saved him. It saved me, too, and if you're reading these pages it probably saved you. Addiction is one of the only illnesses out there that lies to its sufferers and tells them that they're not sick when—in truth—they're dying.

But it's natural, and sane, to want to escape such suffering. That's the original urge that drives us to use drugs, and to heal, Perkins says, we have to accept that truth. Meditation lets us practice acceptance.

"The ground of our addiction is the brilliant sanity of not wanting to suffer. It's *sane* not to want to suffer," he says. "We're just not skillful in how we try not to suffer. And there's a path that can help us see the suffering more directly and create more space around our impulses so we can deal more skillfully with our suffering."

He's expressing the same ideas as Britton and Brewer are. He's just using different words, different images, different tools.

Perkins said he'd been practicing meditation for some years before experiencing the stunning realization that his body was sitting still inside meditation. "I can viscerally remember staffing a three-month meditation program in Colorado and finally, for the first time, realizing, 'I'm sitting here!—like, *physically here!*' It felt at that moment like, 'Oh my god, all this time I've only been meditating *in my head.*'"

Not everybody, however, is able to sit still. In fact, the body doesn't have to perform meditation only on a cushion or a bench. Yoga, which is now a staple of gyms and fitness centers coast to coast, originated in India as a physical discipline—like sitting—to unite the body and mind. "One of the yoga sutras talks about taming the revolutions of the mind—our broken, diseased thoughts, that 'stinking thinking,'" says my friend Jenn, the new mom and Carnegie Mellon neuroscience lab worker who teaches yoga. "So I always think about those diseased thinking patterns. And whether you do it through meditation, which is yoga . . .'"

"Wait, what?" I ask. "Meditation *is* yoga?"

"Oh yeah," she says. "They're inseparable. And when somebody comes into a yoga practice and they talk about just doing physical postures— yeah, that's cool, but the real purpose is to find that place of calming the mind. It's *exactly* the same thing as meditation."

Jenn is a physically beautiful woman with huge brown eyes, a full-lipped smile, and an open face that comes not just from her innately open personality but also from the peace she derives from her meditative practice. Her openness allows her to connect with people: She has a gazillion Facebook friends and LinkedIn connections; she is comfortable cold-calling anyone, whether the person is a government official, a celebrity, or a newly sober woman from a local halfway house, where she volunteers regularly, offering free yoga training. At first I thought this ability to connect was just a "gift" she has—and partly it is. But as Willoughby Britton suggests, we can also practice these skills, and Jenn's ability to connect is borne of humility that's a result of her yoga practice. She can call on people, she can reach out, because she *practices* reaching out. "I think I blocked that connection when I drank," she says. "That connection was so overwhelming for me that I didn't know how to handle it. When I was drinking, connecting with people became all about myself, with a very small 's.' I was so self-seeking that I did nice things for people, but there was always an ulterior motive. So it wasn't like I was really generous."

During her volunteer trainings at the Pennsylvania Organization for Women in Early Recovery (POWER) House, Jenn leads the residents through a meditation that asks them to imagine their minds are like dark oceans during a storm. "When we first start yoga, or when we first begin to run or bike, our minds are dark, there are like forty-foot waves, you can't see what's in the trough behind the wave till you get to the top," she says. "I always find that if we're able to just sit with our breath, we can sort of be—this sounds so cheesy and cliché—but we're able to roll with the waves and become part of the ocean instead of fighting our way ahead, resisting, and crashing." We no longer fight anyone or anything.

"So we stay tethered to our breath," she says, "and it becomes our anchor, literally. The practice for these women in early recovery—and really for me on a daily basis—is to come back to the breath and understand what's happening in my body. Because when we want to use, it's usually because we have uncomfortable feelings in our bodies. If I can help people to allow themselves to get in touch with those feelings, sit with their breath—just feel embodied—they're able to understand what's happening in their bodies, and before they escalate to the point of using, they're able to just back off and be present and anchored in this moment."

Knowing the nature of the human body not just from a "yogic" stand-point but also from her work in the neuroscience lab, Jenn brings an understanding of the high degree of flexibility—"plasticity"—of the human mind and body. But practice is not like a pill you swallow that does the work for you. Practice takes work. "We have the power to change our minds, and mindfulness becomes our anchor—whatever practice you use to get there," Jenn says. "I think it's the most valuable tool we have. It's the tool we most easily forget."

Mindfulness can help us discern whether we're using chemicals or en-gaging in behaviors in addictive or obsessional ways, and people achieve mindfulness in a variety of ways. Nicole, the former Division 1 runner for Syracuse who is now a personal trainer and manages a gym, says her mindfulness practice has allowed her to sleep more deeply and feel more rested as a direct result of toning down her self-criticism. "Part of my re-covery work for the past six months has been strengthening the voice of my real self and quieting the other voice that wants to drive me into the ground," she tells me. "Just being aware, in any given moment of my life: *Is it my true voice or is it the other voice?*

"And I've always thought that I'm just an early morning person. I sleep pretty well, but even on weekends, I'm up at seven o'clock after a fit-ful, restless sleep. I hit the ground running every day. But just recently I've been sleeping 'til nine. And I'm thinking, *Is this a thyroid thing? Is there something wrong?* But I realized that I'm quieting this driving voice. Once I'm aware of it, it's like, *Shut up. I've had enough of you today. I need to take a rest.*"

She uses yoga's practice of awareness of the breath to help her focus on her motivations. The daily practice helps her align her will with her own personal well-being. "I ask myself, 'Why am I exercising today? Because it makes me feel better and it's a gift to myself? Or is it an es-cape?' Because it could be either. It's just that constant recommitment to myself, every day."

Her mindfulness practice has also helped her find deeper intimacy in close relationships. Meditation and yoga allow her to sit with the discomfort and fear of intimacy and to discern whether she's using her sexuality as a way to validate herself—a way to get high—or to grow closer to another human being. "I used to find men who would fall in love with me and make me the center of their universe, and that would make me feel really good. Then I'd wake up one morning and think *I don't even really love this person.* I only attained joy and pleasure after developing intimacy. It took a long time in my life to get to the point where I was ready to be vulnerable with my husband."

For Arielle, the steady pumping of the pedals on her bike allows her, she says, to be quiet in her body. "I ride because cycling offers me a chance to be quiet, to be in my body, to be rhythmic for a few moments every single day," she says. "This solitude, while surrounded by others, allows me to do my best thinking. It's the time when I feel connected to myself, where no screens or duties are allowed." She cycles to and from work in Seattle—everywhere she goes, in fact, through wet Pacific Northwest weather—and she says it's not just "an exercise in physical achievement, conquering fears, or simple transportation. It's a state of being where I feel authentically myself—and no matter how many times I worry about my safety, I wouldn't give that up for the world."

During this practice of pedaling her body everywhere, through all kinds of weather, Arielle realized a central truth of recovery: that her body is always in the present moment. "I think about this: I can't just go into the future or live in the past. My body is always right here in reality." Right here in Truth. Arielle climbs walls and mountains, she hikes through mud and snow, and she says, "Doing really hard physical things hurts, so I think about my body a lot, and that anchors me to the present moment."

Does she think she's addicted to pain, to constant challenge, to achievement? Arielle continually posts photos on Instagram from the peaks she climbs in the Cascade range. She delves into books about mountaineers who climb trails 18,000 feet in elevation. "Once you get that high, you usually die eventually," she says, and I'm aware of the play on the word "high." She is constantly scanning the horizon for the next goal. Checking in with someone about her motivations helps her stay realistic. Her mother, who works as an acupuncturist and fed her "really good wholesome food" when she was growing up, helps Arielle stay mindful about the challenges she sets for herself. "I told my mom I signed up for this bike ride from Seattle to Portland in July—it's two hundred miles and you can do it in two days or one day. I'm training for the one-day trip, and she was like, *What the hell? You just really like being in pain and torturing yourself.* I've been thinking about that this week." This is also mindfulness practice: small acts of awareness, of clear perception and understanding, during each day.

About three years out of detox, an insight I never expected to have gradually dawned on me: I needed a dog.

I did my best not to pay attention to this awareness because, as far as I was concerned, it was complete sentimental bollocks and a total mistake: how would I train a dog? I had never owned a dog. Plus, it was going to cost me money, which was never good. Cats are much more low-maintenance, and I'd always been a cat person. I'd owned cats since I was a little girl and my family adopted Ethel from the Humane Society shelter on Hamilton Avenue in Homewood, the neighborhood John Edgar Wideman wrote about in his memoir *Brothers and Keepers*: a rough part of town for a rough cat. Ethel slept on a scrap of carpet in the basement and patrolled the yard outside our lonely suburban house, closing firm jowls on the mouse population. When I was fourteen, Ethel ran away. The woman who played organ for the church told my mother she had a cat with a litter of orange kittens, and she said we could pick one out. So Penny came to live with us. Penny was an altogether different animal. She purred when she slept on my bed. It was the first time I'd ever experienced an animal making a sound of contentment in response to my presence, and I know now that the waterfall of warmth I felt flooding through my chest was a result of oxytocin, the body's bonding hormone, cascading underneath my skin. (There are some theories out there that indicate people with addiction have precious little oxytocin going on—the more bonding we can do, the better.) When I grew up and moved into my first apartment, an advertising sales guy I worked with in my newsroom said he and his wife had found a kitten while spotting deer on a country road, and that was how I acquired Sully, who lived with me for almost twenty years.

But a dog? Dogs (said my mother, who was wrong about a lot of stuff, but whose wrong ideas have persisted as scary fairy tales in my mind) were dirty; you had to bathe them. They weren't smart enough to wash themselves like cats could. If they couldn't wash themselves, they automatically smelled bad. If they smelled bad, they would make your house smell bad. They were dumb—you had to tie them up so they wouldn't run away, because, unlike cats, who were smart, dogs couldn't find their own way home. They couldn't even take care of themselves for a day or so if you wanted to go away.

Worst of all, you had to walk them.

I mean, where would we ever have walked a dog? I grew up in Strip-Mall Land, where nobody ever walked anywhere. If you wanted anything in the suburbs, you got in the car and drove a minimum of a mile, a distance that you couldn't walk because there were no sidewalks or even shoulders on the road, and if you tried to walk, you'd get yourself killed by a pickup or a coal truck.

Country kids owned dogs, of course. These were the kids who took off for Potter County (with their dads, dogs, and guns) for opening day of deer season. Then there were city kids, like my cousins, who owned dogs. These kids had roads with sidewalks, so they could walk their dogs. . . . Of course I'm playing with you. There were also scads of suburban kids who could walk their dogs because they lived in normal housing plans, what most people in America called "neighborhoods," which had either sidewalks or roads on which they wouldn't get killed if they walked on them. And anyhow, I'd even *known* a few suburban people who loved dogs. My college boyfriend Dave, for example, who taught me to play tennis, and who also lived in Strip-Mall Land, had two Samoyed dogs that ran to the door every time he came home, because they could pick out his voice. But I always thought they seemed to see the word "cat" written on my forehead, because they never came to the door for me. (I now think, *Why would they?*—I was afraid of them. I didn't know how *not* to be afraid. At the time, as usual, I felt stupid and left out.)

About a year after I detoxed, I met my friend Petra and her two-year-old yellow Labrador, Ginger. Yellow Labradors are the most popular dog in America. They are smart, obedient (if well-trained), and generally friendly and calm. As I got to know Petra better, I visited her house more often. Ginger was the first dog in my life who ever came to the door when she heard my voice. She has that yellow Lab face with the warm deep-brown eyes and the black-rimmed mouth that looks like she's smiling.

"She *is* smiling!" Petra would say, laughing. "Dogs smile."

Whatever. I waited for Ginger to be smelly and stupid. But Ginger always smelled like Petra's perfume, so she reminded me of Petra, and of course, this made me kiss her head. Pretty soon I wasn't just kissing her head, I was rubbing my face through her hair and putting my arms around her big body, plus talking to her in that quasi baby voice that people use to talk to their dogs. And she wasn't even my dog.

Although Ginger's owners sometimes say she's "bred for beauty and not for brains," Ginger ain't dumb. Ginger eventually began to do things like plant her head on my knee and stare at me with those seal eyes until I petted her, or bring me her ball so I could throw it, or curl her body next to mine on the couch while we were watching a movie. And my body would respond: I'd feel that warm flood that I'd felt when Penny purred against my neck. No wonder that many studies (and perennial headlines) tell us that people with dogs live longer than those without. And it's not just because of the beneficial effects of the bonding hormone, the "good chemicals," which are significant.

It's also because, yes, dogs demand to be walked.

They need to be walked not because, as my mother seemed to believe, they're "stupid" and can't get their ya-yas out by climbing trees the way cats can. It's because dogs are pack animals. For their own peace of mind and mental health—just to feel normal—they need to perceive their bodies being led through their world by their Top Dog at least once each day. Or so I've been told.

Interesting, because humans are also pack animals—which is one reason why *Canis lupus* and *Homo sapiens* have evolved together so harmoniously throughout the millennia.

So I'd spend some time with Ginger, she'd love me up and make my body rain oxytocin, and I'd kiss her dog face—something I never, ever imagined doing, putting my Clean Human Lips on a dog's big furry face with its wet nose and slimy tongue—but Ginger was starting to look less to me like a "dog" and more like big nice blonde person who would re-cline on the couch and let me hug her for hours. And it would come time for me to go home, and I'd feel like I'd want to sneak Ginger in the car with me. I'd go about my days and find my mind engaging in ideas of *Should my dog be light-colored or dark-colored, a boy or girl?* and *Where in the kitchen will the dog bowl go?* and *What will I do about the hair that the dog will shed all over the floor?*

And of course: *Where will I walk the dog?* Because I work at home. Some days I never even leave the house. The dog, I imagined, would nudge me out into the world. Into the flow of life.

These ideas scared me so much that you'd have thought I was con-sidering where to put my new baby *T. rex.* These are the kinds of ideas and intuitions normal people have all the time—to people without drug addictions, these thoughts just mean simple things like, *I want a dog*—but they rocked my world, they portended *change,* and if I had still been using, I would have drugged them away. I'm sure my meditative prac-tice helped me recognize that these fantasies constituted a normal de-sire to have a dog and an ability to see that I could commit to taking care of one. At the very least, they convinced me to talk to Petra, who assured me I was indeed normal, and who was overjoyed to volunteer to help me train a puppy. "Get a puppy," she said, "and I can guarantee you a good re-sult." So in April 2012, I finally surrendered to the increasing frequency of these fantasies and, Bang, I just happened to come across a litter of rescue puppies, from which I acquired my black Lab-mix girlie.

I named her Flo. She has grown to be forty-five pounds—all black, with a kind of whippet-like high waist and that extra skin that Labradors carry around their neck. Plus the seal-like waterproof jet-black Lab hair. As I write this, she's sleeping on the bed at my feet.

Flo. I figured if I were going to be saying a dog's name several dozen times a day, why not make it a statement that would remind me to do something productive? Flo. Flow. Go with the flow.

Or as Janice told me so often, simply, "Accept, then move."

Almost nothing reminds me of the fact that awareness is the result of simple practice more than walking Flo. Like meditation, walking Flo is just a job that needs to be done. In fact, walking Flo can be a meditation of its own. I sometimes use my time moving my body with Flo's to open my eyes and notice my own neighborhood, a landscape that, because I've lived here for twenty years, I thought I knew inside out. Each time I put the leash on Flo, I put on my "beginner's mind," and I catch sights I'd ignored, dismissed, overlooked—street art, falling-down masonry, painted architecture, abandoned buildings, gardens, weeds, wildflowers, piles of trash, corners of beauty or destruction or both. I also train Flo, who is afraid of a few things as disparate as buses and umbrellas. I urge her to keep moving through the parts of life that scare her, and in training Flo, I train my mind in confidence and authority and my body in fitness. It's usually tedious, often tiring, sometimes (as when I'm anemic) a real drag for which I have to ask for help.

And then, because I ask, and because they care about me and Flo, people come and help.

And god, how Flo loves me. She just *loooves* me. Yeah, I let her lick my face, which I never thought I'd let any dog do. She slept on my feet for most of the past long, hard winter. When I scratch her ears, she moans these deep little moans I think of as her "eargasms."

And Petra's right: Flo smiles at me.

None of this would have happened without my practicing meditation.

I have a jade pendant of a goddess I sometimes wear around my neck that reminds me to listen to these kinds of intuitions. The Chinese call this goddess Guan Yin. In India, they call her Avalokitesvara, the Buddha of Compassion. She sits on a lotus flower and holds a bottle representing the tears that people the world over have cried—are crying, right now. This pendant came to me from my friend Tony, a guy with whom I used to study a Korean form of yoga. Tony learned this form in Seoul, a place he's frequently visited and where his yoga master lives. Tony is serious about his practice, and he took equal seriousness in teaching me. At one point, back in the early 2000s, I reached a level of proficiency such that Tony took the time, on one of his visits to Seoul, to enter my name into a registry of people who were proficient in this form. He brought me back a uniform with an official patch on it.

He also brought me the jade pendant. When he gave it to me, he said it had been carved during the Song Dynasty. I had no clue when the Song Dynasty took place, so I looked it up and found it ran from the years 960 to 1279, which meant this jade carving is anywhere from seven hundred to more than one thousand years old. The pendant is about two-and-a-half inches long and a little more than an inch wide. It's strung on a piece of fine natural brown leather thong with a red wooden bead threaded near the hole at the top.

The stone heats up when it lies next to the skin over my breastbone.

The Buddha of Compassion, Tony told me, is "She who hears the cries of the world."

When Tony gave me this pendant, I sort of didn't believe him that it was a thousand years old, because who gives somebody a thousand-year-old pendant? No, I mean who gives *me* a thousand-year-old pendant? I was taking OxyContin at the time. I remember this because I had agreed, as part of my practice, to get up before sunrise and carry out the long series of prescribed exercises that was the foundation of this practice, and I was supposed to do it on an empty stomach, but I always took the drug first. By then my body was dependent on the drug, my mind was dependent on the drug, I was incapable of carrying out the exercises, or doing anything really, without Taking Something. I tried, and I couldn't do it: I'd always give up and pop one of the purple tablets out of the bubble pack, crunch it up, and swallow. And of course, during the practice, I could feel the drug taking effect, because my whole body and mind were attuned to this feeling. The drug dominated my awareness. Eventually, my inability to practice without taking drugs made me feel like a fraud and a failure, and I quit—the practice, not the drugs. In other words, I chose drugs over this discipline that was designed to help me be healthier and more mindful. I also put drugs in front of my friendship with Tony. And I packed up the jade and I never wore it again—until I detoxed.

When I was about three or four months out of detox, I asked Tony to come to lunch with me. I hadn't seen him in a while, and at a certain point during our lunch, I think it became clear to him that I'd asked him there to listen to me thank him for being so kind to me and to tell him I thought I'd hurt him by privileging drugs over our friendship. I didn't feel right about wearing his gift without telling Tony I'd taken drugs during the whole time I was working with him—something I'd assiduously hidden from him, as I tried to hide it from everyone. He sat there under the recessed spotlights in the Middle Eastern restaurant. His hair was still very short, almost shaved, and he was wearing a jacket and tie, but he carried himself as though he were wearing a kameez tunic, maybe, and no shoes. I felt as though he were peering inside my skull as he suggested that, by holding this conversation with him, perhaps I was trying to accomplish too much in too short a time and that I have a way of putting pressure on myself. I wish I had a dollar for every time anyone has ever told me I'm hard on myself. I used drugs to try to stifle that hard-assed voice.

"You've done something that not many people in the world ever manage to do," he said. "You've gotten yourself off these drugs. Many people spend the rest of their lives either on drugs like that or trying to get off and failing over and over again."

"What do you think makes the difference?" I asked. "Why could I quit and my parents couldn't?" In the early days of my recovery, this question eclipsed lots of others.

"I think it's being able to see oneself as an addict," he said. "Maybe it's being able to see oneself at all. Your parents couldn't see themselves. They had no ability to get outside themselves and look at what they were doing."

No mindfulness, very little awareness. Just knowing what to do in the moment. Trying to choose the right action at the right time: response. "Respond" comes from the Latin root meaning "to pledge." To commit, promise, again. We may not follow through on our promises, but we can try again. The word carries an implication of intention and hope.

The pendant reminds me to respond with compassion. The word "compassion" doesn't mean simply "to feel with"—it means "to suffer with." What makes people in recovery pick up the phone when it rings with another person in recovery on the other end is the willingness to suffer with that person. Dollars to donuts (as my mother was fond of saying), a "program call" is not going to be News of the Awesome. It's going to be "I lost my job," "My boyfriend cheated on me," "My apartment got burgled and they took all my jewelry," "My dad has cancer," "I'm depressed/sad/angry/afraid and I'm hungry/angry/lonely/tired." Basically, "I Want To Use." I pick up the phone when I know it's going to be one of these stories of suffering, because other people have picked up the phone when I've called with my own stories of suffering. It's payback. Karma. Practice.

As I was finishing this book, my friend Alice, seventy-seven, who used to drink and take painkillers and has been sober for thirty-odd years, came back from visiting her sister who had a stem-cell transplant. "This is my baby sister," Alice tells me. "She's sixty-eight. I could always call her for everything—but of course I can't right now." Alice says during her visit she stayed near the hospital in low-cost family housing that was uncomfortable. And even though drinking was prohibited on the property, one of the other women kept inviting Alice to join her on the porch for a glass of wine. This woman also told Alice that she had plenty of Ambien to share if Alice couldn't sleep. As noted earlier, Ambien, or zolpidem, is a sedative-hypnotic used as a sleep aid; it has a mechanism of action similar to benzodiazepines such as Valium and Xanax, and since it acts on the same receptors, it can be abused.

Alice declined both the wine and the pills. "Being there for my sister saved me," she says.

"Helping her helped you?" I ask.

"I wasn't really *helping* her," she says. "I was just sitting there. Being with her. And if I'd taken that stuff, it wouldn't have been me there with her." Alice would have abandoned herself.

"I can't have Just A Little Wine. I can't have Just A Little Ambien," Alice says. "What I realized was that when I was drinking and using drugs, life became an illusion. And it didn't take very long for the illusion to set in and take over all of my life. The illusion"—or the delusion, as I think of it—"was so pervasive that it completely cut me off from what was happening in my life and from people's reactions to what I was doing."

It cut her off from "reality." From the truth.

She says she was glad to be able to tell the woman she didn't want any wine or pills, to climb the stairs to her "stinky little room" as she called it, and then to fall asleep.

"And then to wake up as myself."

"That's what recovery is about, right?" I say to her. "Waking up?—as yourself."

"Yeah," she says—in her slight accent, it comes out more as *ja*—and as she regards me, I look closely at her face, her seventy-seven-year-old face written beautifully with years of care, with sun damage and thinning eyebrows and skin that pools underneath pale eyes that have seen nearly eight decades of life, children, grandchildren, two husbands, one divorce, the second husband the love of her life dead after just eight years of marriage. Recovery does not promise beauty or riches, everlasting affection and security or even sustained peace of mind. It promises that we'll be able to negotiate one day—this one—in our right minds, awake. We get good at what we practice.

She sighs. We put our arms around each other and I put my palm on the back of her neck—because I've discovered that when I do that, something loosens in the other person's body and they can feel the fact that I'm holding their body in my arms. Then she takes my face between her hands and presses her lips firmly and slowly to my forehead.

"Waking up is tiresome and tiring," she says. "It's rewarding. It's necessary."

Some Guidelines

Here are some guidelines to follow as you begin or continue to awaken the permanent home that is your mind and body:

- Meditation is a whole-body physical practice—it doesn't just happen inside the head.
- Meditation is exercise for the executive brain. It wakes up the prefrontal cortex, which was disabled by drug use, and gives it greater control over the midbrain's cravings, which meditation tones down.

- Meditating two minutes per day may not seem like a lot, but it's more helpful than meditating zero minutes per day.
- We're not trying to "feel" anything in particular during meditation or prayer. What's valuable is the discipline of practicing regularly.
- Preliminary research suggests that prayer accomplishes the same results meditation does.

References

Introduction

Whyte, David. *Midlife and the Great Unknown: Finding Courage and Clarity through Poetry*. Louisville, Colo.: Sounds True Audio, 2003.

Chapter 1

Associated Press, "'Killer Heroin' Blamed in Fatal Overdoses." February 16, 2014. Accessed May 5, 2014. www.nbcnews.com/news/us-news/killer-heroin -blamed-fatal-overdoses-n31801.

Nutt, David J., Leslie A. King, Lawrence D. Phillips, on behalf of the Independent Scientific Committee on Drugs. "Drug Harms in the UK: A Multicriteria Decision Analysis." *The Lancet* 376 (2010): 1558–65.

Maté, Gabor. *In the Realm of Hungry Ghosts: Close Encounters with Addiction*. Berkeley, Calif.: North Atlantic Books, 2010.

National Council on Alcoholism and Drug Dependence Inc. (NCADD), FAQs/ Facts. Accessed May 5, 2014. www.ncadd.org/index.php?option=com_ content&view=category&layout=blog&id=89&Itemid=308.

Peart, R. F. "The Benzodiazephines: Toxicity, Cognitive Impairment, Long-Term Damage and the Post Withdrawal Syndrome." Accessed May 5, 2014. www.benzo.org.uk/vot4.htm.

Emanuele, Mary Ann, and Nicholas Emanuele. "Alcohol and the Male Repro-ductive System." A publication of the National Institute on Alcohol Abuse and Alcoholism (NIAAA). http://pubs.niaaa.nih.gov/publications /arh25-4/282-287.htm.

Emanuele, Mary Ann, Frederick Wezeman, and Nicholas Emanuele. "Alcohol's Effects on Female Reproductive Function." A publication of the NIAAA. Accessed May 5, 2014. http://pubs.niaaa.nih.gov/publications/arh26-4 /274-281.htm.

"Faces of Meth." Accessed May 5, 2014. www.facesofmeth.us/main.htm.

NIAAA, "Alcohol Facts and Statistics." Accessed May 5, 2014. www.niaaa.nih .gov/alcohol-health/overview-alcohol-consumption/ alcohol-facts-and-statistics.

Zhong, Wenjun, et al. "Age and Sex Patterns of Drug Prescribing in a Defined American Population." *Mayo Clinic Proceedings* 88 (7) (July 2013): 697–707. Accessed May 5, 2014. www.mayoclinicproceedings.org/article /S0025-6196(13)00357-1/abstract.

Chapter 2

Lieberman, Daniel. "To Move Is Human." *New York Times,* June 24, 2013. Accessed May 5, 2014. www.nytimes.com/roomfordebate/2013/06/24 /addicted-to-endorphins/moving-the-human-body-is-a-necessity-and -rarely-an-addiction.

Lieberman, Daniel. *The Story of the Human Body: Evolution, Health, and Disease.* New York: Pantheon, 2013.

Clinton Foundation 2014 Health Matters Conference, Mental Health & Prescription Drug Abuse Prevention Panel. Accessed May 5, 2014. http://new.livestream.com/clintonfoundationus/healthmatters2014 /videos/39640376.

Dietrich, Alexander, and Wayne F. McDaniel. "Endocannabinoids and Exercise." *British Journal of Sports Medicine* 38 (2004): 536–41.

Raichlen, David A., et al. "Wired to Run: Exercise-Induced Endocannabinoid Signaling in Humans and Cursorial Mammals with Implications for the 'Runner's High.'" *Journal of Experimental Biology* 215 (2012):1331–36.

Blumenthal, J. A., et al. "Is Exercise a Viable Treatment for Depression?" *American College of Sports Medicine's Health Fitness Journal* 16 (4) (2012): 14–21.

CNN Heroes 2012. "Scott Strode, Community Crusader." February 9, 2012. Accessed May 5, 2014. www.cnn.com/SPECIALS/cnn.heroes/2012.heroes /scott.strode.html.

Niemeyer, Shane, with Gary Brozek. *The Hurt Artist: My Journey from Suicidal Junkie to Ironman.* New York: Thomas Dunne Books, 2014.

Chapter 3

DesMaisons, Kathleen. *Potatoes Not Prozac: Solutions for Sugar Sensitivity.*
New York: Simon & Schuster, 2008, chapter 9.

Avena, Nicole M., Pedro Rada, and Bartley G. Hoebel. "Evidence for Sugar
Addiction: Behavioral and Neurochemical Effects of Intermittent, Excessive
Sugar Intake." *Neuroscience Biobehavioral Review* 32(1) (2008): 20–39.

Ketcham, Katherine, and L. Ann Mueller, M.D. *Eating Right to Live Sober:
A Comprehensive Guide to Alcoholism and Nutrition.* Seattle: Madrona
Publishers, 1983.

Helliker, Kevin. "Why Runners Can't Eat Whatever They Want." *Wall Street
Journal,* March 26, 2014. Accessed May 5, 2014. http://online.wsj.com
/news/articles/SB10001424052702303949704579461381883678174
?mg=reno64-wsj&url=http%3A%2F%2Fonline.wsj.com%2Farticle%2
FSB10001424052702303949704579461381883678174.html.

Cowan, J., and C. Devine. "Food, Eating and Weight Concerns of Men in
Recovery from Substance Addiction." *Appetite* 2007, 50 (1) (2008): 33–42.

Dwyer, Jim. "Truth and a Prize Emerge from Lies about Hoffman." *New York
Times,* February 25, 2014. Accessed May 5, 2014. www.nytimes.com/2014
/02/26/nyregion/after-a-deluge-of-fiction-a-friend-of-hoffmans-insists-on
-the-truth.html.

Perlmutter, David, with Kristin Loberg. *Grain Brain: The Surprising Truth
about Wheat, Carbs, and Sugar—Your Brain's Silent Killers.* New York:
Little, Brown, 2013.

Hamblin, James. "This Is Your Brain on Gluten." *The Atlantic,* December 20,
2013. Accessed May 5, 2014. www.theatlantic.com/health/archive/2013/12
/this-is-your-brain-on-gluten/282550.

Pollan, Michael. *Food Rules: An Eater's Manual.* New York: Penguin, 2009.

Wallace, David Foster. "Transcription of the 2005 Kenyon Commencement
Address" delivered May 21, 2005. Accessed May 5, 2014. http://web.ics
.purdue.edu/~drkelly/DFWKenyonAddress2005.pdf.

Chapter 4

Carlin, George. *Brain Droppings.* New York: Hyperion, 1997.

Johnson, K. "The Effects of Maternal Stress and Anxiety during Pregnancy."
Maternal Substance Abuse and Child Development Project, Emory University

School of Medicine Department of Psychiatry and Behavioral Sciences. Accessed May 5, 2014. www.psychiatry.emory.edu/PROGRAMS/GADrug /Feature%20Articles/Mothers/The%20effects%20of%20maternal%20 stress%20and%20anxiety%20during%20pregnancy%20(mot07).pdf.

2013 Sleep in America Poll: Exercise and Sleep. Arlington, Va.: National Sleep Foundation, 2013.

Wong, Maria M., et al. "Sleep Problems in Early Childhood and Early Onset of Alcohol and Other Drug Use in Adolescence." *Alcoholism: Clinical and Experimental Research* 28 (4) (2004): 578–87.

Clegg, Bill. *Portrait of an Addict as a Young Man: A Memoir.* New York: Little Brown, 2010.

Amnesty International Public Statement, April 3, 2014. http://www.amnesty .eu/content/assets/Reports/030414_cia_us_public_statement.pdf.

Zhang Jing, et al. "Extended Wakefulness: Compromised Metabolics in and Degeneration of Locus Ceruleus Neurons." *The Journal of Neuroscience* 34 (12) (2014): 4418–31.

Jordania, Joseph. *Why Do People Sing? Music in Human Evolution.* Tblisi, Georgia: Logos, 2011.

Maté, Gabor. *In the Realm of Hungry Ghosts: Close Encounters with Addiction.* Berkeley, Calif.: North Atlantic Books, 2010.

American Society of Addiction Medicine. "Public Policy Statement: Definition of Addiction." Accessed May 5, 2014. www.asam.org/for-the-public /definition-of-addiction.

Matesa, Jennifer, with Jed Bickman. "A New View of Addiction Stirs Up a Scientific Storm." *The Fix,* August 16, 2011. Accessed May 5, 2014. www.thefix.com/content/addiction-gets-medical-makeover8004.

Centers for Disease Control and Prevention. "Injury Prevention and Control: Adverse Childhood Experiences (ACE) Study." Accessed May 5, 2014. www.cdc.gov/ace.

Miller, Alice. *The Drama of the Gifted Child: The Search for the True Self.* New York: Basic Books, 1981.

Lamott, Anne. "Why I Hate Mother's Day." *Salon.* May 8, 2010. Accessed May 5, 2014. www.salon.com/2010/05/08/hate_mothers_day_anne_lamott.

Chapter 5

McCauley, Kevin. *Pleasure Unwoven: An Explanation of the Brain Disease of Addiction* (DVD). Salt Lake City, Utah: The Institute for Addiction Study, 2010.

King, Stephen. *On Writing: A Memoir of the Craft.* New York: Scribner, 1999.

Colamerco, Stephen, and Joshua S. Coren. "Opioid-Induced Endocrinopathy." *The Journal of the American Osteopathic Association* 209 (2009): 20–25.

Clegg, Bill. *Portrait of an Addict as a Young Man: A Memoir.* New York: Little Brown, 2010.

Clegg, Bill. *Ninety Days: A Memoir of Recovery.* New York: Back Bay Books, 2013.

Brecher, Edward M., and editors of *Consumer Reports Magazine*, 1972. "Effects of Opium, Morphine, and Heroin on Addicts" in *The Consumers Union Report on Licit and Illicit Drugs.* Schaffer Library of Drug Policy. Accessed May 5, 2014. www.druglibrary.org/schaffer/library/studies/cu/cu4.html.

Garfield Barbach, Lonnie. *For Yourself: The Fulfillment of Female Sexuality.* New York: Doubleday, 1975.

On Being with Krista Tippett. "Sherwin Nuland—The Biology of the Spirit." Recorded interview, March 6, 2014. Accessed May 5, 2014. www.onbeing.org/program/biology-spirit/184.

Chapter 6

Pinola, Melanie. "Meditation Can Improve Your Memory, Focus, and Productivity at Work." *Lifehacker,* July 10, 2012. Accessed May 5, 2014. http://lifehacker.com/5924792/meditation-can-improve-your-memory-focus-and-productivity-at-work.

Confino, Jo. "Google Seeks Out Wisdom of Zen Master Thich Nhat Hanh." *The Guardian,* September 5, 2013. Accessed May 5, 2014. www.theguardian.com/sustainable-business/global-technology-ceos-wisdom-zen-master-thich-nhat-hanh.

TEDx Talks. "TEDxBrown University—Willoughby Britton—Why a Neuroscientist Would Study Meditation." Accessed May 5, 2014. www.youtube.com/watch?v=TR8TjCncvIw.

Britton, Willoughby B., et al. "Awakening Is Not a Metaphor: The Effects of Buddhist Meditation Practices on Basic Wakefulness." *Annals of the New York Academy of Sciences* 1307 (2014): 64–81.

Brewer, Judson A., et al. "Mindfulness Training for Smoking Cessation: Results from a Randomized Controlled Trial." *Drug and Alcohol Dependence* 119 (2011): 72–80.

Dakwar, Elias, and Frances R. Levin. "The Emerging Role of Meditation in Addressing Psychiatric Illness, with a Focus on Substance Use Disorders." *Harvard Review of Psychiatry* 17 (4) (2009): 254–67.

Piver, Susan. The Open Heart Project. Accessed May 5, 2014. http://susanpiver .com/open-heart-project.

Wideman, John Edgar. *Brothers and Keepers.* New York: Holt, Rinehart and Winston, 1984.

Fortini, Amanda. "Mary Karr: The Art of Memoir No. 1." *Paris Review,* Winter 2009. Accessed May 5, 2014. www.theparisreview.org/interviews/5992 /the-art-of-memoir-no-1-mary-karr.

Lamott, Anne. *Help, Thanks, Wow: The Three Essential Prayers.* New York: Riverhead, 2012.

Brown, Brené. "The Power of Vulnerability." Accessed May 5, 2014. http:// www.ted.com/talks/brene_brown_on_vulnerability.

Brown, Brené. *The Gifts of Imperfection: Let Go of Who You Think You're Supposed to Be and Embrace Who You Are.* Center City, Minnesota: Hazelden, 2010.

Servan-Schreiber, David. *The Instinct to Heal: Curing Depression, Anxiety, and Stress Without Drugs and Without Talk Therapy.* Emmaus, Pa.: Rodale Books, 2004.

About the Author

Jennifer Matesa has written about health and life transformation for more than twenty years, including two previously published books, *Navel-Gazing: The Days and Nights of a Mother in the Making*, chosen by Lamaze International as a Top-Ten pregnancy and childbirth resource, and *Knowing Stephanie*, a biography of a young breast cancer patient. In 2010 she established the popular blog *Guinevere Gets Sober* (www .guineveregetssober.com), for which she has interviewed many scientists, practitioners, authors, and ordinary folks with fascinating stories about recovering from addiction. She has contributed journalistic coverage of addiction to many publications, and for many years she has taught writing at the University of Pittsburgh. Since 2012 she has regularly educated groups of medical students about ways to prevent, identify, and respond to addiction in their patients. In 2013 she was awarded a yearlong fellowship with the federal Substance Abuse and Mental Health Services Administration (SAMHSA) in recognition of her public education about the human potential to heal.

Also of Interest

by Thérèse Jacobs-Stewart

Mindfulness and the 12 Steps

Living Recovery in the Present Moment

With the artistry of a memoirist, Jacobs-Stewart draws on her personal story and an impressive range of knowledge in psychology, spirituality, and the Twelve Steps to show us the way out of the morass of pain and confusion that addiction creates.
Order No. 2862; ebook EB2862

by Allen Berger, Ph.D.

12 Stupid Things That Mess Up Recovery

Avoiding Relapse through Self-Awareness and Right Action

To grow in recovery, we must grow up emotionally. This means getting honest with ourselves and facing up to the self-defeating thoughts and actions that put our sobriety at risk—patterns such as not making amends; using the program to try to become perfect; and believing that life should be easy. Discover the twelve most common recovery-sabotaging attitudes—and the tools for working through them in daily life.
Order No. 3001; ebook EB3001

12 Smart Things to Do When the Booze and Drugs Are Gone

Choosing Emotional Sobriety through Self-Awareness and Right Action

Whether we call it dry-drunk syndrome or white-knuckle sobriety, it's that stage in recovery when we realize that "putting the plug in the jug" isn't enough. The next step is taking responsibility for the emotional immaturity that fuels our addictive personality. Berger outlines twelve hallmarks of emotional sobriety that, when practiced, give people the confidence to be accountable for their behavior, ask for what they want and need, and grow and develop a deeper trust in the process of life.
Order No. 2864; ebook EB2864